MW00331712

IMAGES
of America

SAN LORENZO

MEEK MANSION FOUNTAIN, 1950S. This damaged and inoperable fountain was restored from 1994 to 1996 by volunteer Bob Campisi, a retired plumber and area resident. The Hayward Area Park and Recreation District, owners of the property, located a fountain sketch and one of 12 broken serpent fish to make a mold to replace the two missing vases. Now, as a magnificent working fountain, it highlights the mansion entrance.

ON THE COVER: SAN LORENZO BLACKSMITH SHOP. The first business in 1853 was John Boyle's blacksmith shop. After his death, Henry Smyth, who worked for him, bought the business. The blacksmith and wheelwright shop made plows and wagons, shod horses, and repaired farm equipment and buggies. It employed 30–40 people. Later William Z. Smith, who had been an employee since 1898, rented the shop from Henry Smyth until 1930.

IMAGES
of America

SAN LORENZO

Doris Marciel and the
Hayward Area Historical Society

ARCADIA
PUBLISHING

Published by Arcadia Publishing
Charleston, South Carolina

Library of Congress Catalog Card Number: 2006931278

For all general information contact Arcadia Publishing at:
Telephone 843-853-2070
Fax 843-853-0044
E-mail sales@arcadiapublishing.com
For customer service and orders:
Toll-Free 1-888-313-2665

Visit us on the Internet at www.arcadiapublishing.com

This book is dedicated to my mother, the late Pauline Joseph Marciel, a San Lorenzo native, whose love of history and San Lorenzo was my resource and inspiration to teach San Lorenzo history.

CONTENTS

ACKNOWLEDGMENTS

During the 20 years of teaching and writing articles about my native town, San Lorenzo, I was encouraged, especially by the adult school students, to write a book. When Jim DeMersman, executive director of the Hayward Area Historical Society, arranged to have books published by Arcadia Publishing for Hayward, Castro Valley, and San Lorenzo, I was elated.

I could not have completed the book without the assistance and expertise of Devon Weston as photograph editor and copy manager.

Special thanks to friends and relatives for sharing pictures and memories of San Lorenzo, especially Lola Giannelli, Frank Denevi, Tom Vierra, Loretta Joseph, Ron Smyth, Audrey Lopes, Shirley Scanlon, Pat Davis, Donna McCarty, Claire McKibben, Paula Amaral, Maybelle Rasmussen, Olive Nichimura, Esther Jorgensen, Russell Smyth, Muriel Joseph, Janice Halbach, Elinor Humphrey, Oliver and Veronica Silva, Bonnie Peterson, Lucille Lorge, Mabel Miller, Mary Gonzales, Al Nicolotti, and Mel Peters.

I thank the San Lorenzo Village Homes Association and Esther Jorgensen for lending the scrapbooks and the organizers of the San Lorenzo Unified School District artifacts, Marcene Willard and Barbara Khuns. Special appreciation goes to the staff of the Hayward Area Historical Society for their encouragement, assistance, and access to the extensive photographic files.

INTRODUCTION

"I live in Squatterville," said the newcomer who settled on the north side of the San Lorenzo Creek in 1847. "I came from the East Coast to find gold in the Sierra Mountains of California, but found none. Then I heard about an area by the bay that had rich soil and a good climate. When I got there, I found many others already living in small cabins and tents near the creek. I stayed, and I heard that the land belonged to Spanish owners; now I am a squatter."

Prior to this time, Native Americans lived by the creeks and streams or by freshwater springs. They found food in the creeks and bay, lots of game and animals to eat, trees for shade, fertile soil, and plants to use. Then the Spanish soldiers and padres arrived looking for a location to establish a mission. They selected land south of this area to build Mission San Jose.

When Mexico declared its independence from Spain and took possession of California and the missions, the land was divided into large ranchos and awarded to soldiers or politicians. Acreage measurements were determined using the land's geographic features. They would use trees, creeks, rocks, and roads to form the borders of each rancho. Surveyors had difficulty if the tree died, if there were many rocks, or when they had to decide if it was a "road" or "trail," so borders were difficult to claim.

By 1850, Squatterville had grown and the Californios tried various ways to remove these newcomers. Some squatters, people who settled on land owned by others, bought the land from Castro and Soto and others went to court. Although protected under the Treaty of Guadalupe Hidalgo after California had become a state in 1850, the Californios' land titles still had to go through the American courts to receive a decision. They took years, and the court battles were financially draining. No one knows who suggested the name Squatterville be changed to San Lorenzo in 1854. It might have been taken from the San Lorenzo Creek or Rancho San Lorenzo. Whatever its origins, all San Lorenzo residents thank the early residents for changing the name.

By this time, the town had its first businesses in John Boyle's blacksmith shop; two hotels, The Willows and San Lorenzo House; Shiman's General Store; and a post office. The pioneers organized the Christian Union Society Church, the San Lorenzo Cemetery, and the San Lorenzo Grammar School. Captain Roberts built a wharf and warehouse by the mouth of San Lorenzo Creek to ship farm products to San Francisco. Village Hall, the Pavilion, and San Lorenzo Grove provided recreation for the townspeople and visitors.

The Oakland–San Leandro–Hayward Electric Railway Traction Company line replaced horse trolley cars in the early 1900s, which transported visitors from Oakland and San Francisco. It traveled on East Fourteenth Street to the Junction at 150th Avenue, turned south to current Hesperian Boulevard, and ended at the San Lorenzo Creek Bridge for its return trip back to the Junction. The country people were upset with this new mode of transportation. Their horses were frightened, sometimes running away and overturning buggies with passengers. This resulted in many damage suits against the Traction Company.

San Lorenzo became a wealthy community with large mansions and farms. William Meek had the largest farm and mansion. Other pioneers were John Lewelling, Charles Hathaway, Neal

McConaghy, Capt. William Roberts, John Marlin, Henry Smyth, Clinton King, Otis Webb, Herman Nielson, Charles Stenzel, James Adams, John Henry Gansberger, and William Knox. The grazing fields of the Spanish-Mexican era became the settlers' farmland with potatoes, currants, sugar beets, tomatoes, strawberry rhubarb, and other vegetables, as well as wheat, oats, and barley. Meek and Lewelling brought many grafted fruit trees from Oregon; cherries, pears, apricots, apples, and peaches were some of the most popular. The farmers, with their horses and wagons, would travel to Robert's Landing Road, now Lewelling Boulevard, and wait several hours to unload their farm products onto boats bound for the San Francisco port.

The railroad reduced the need for shipping by boat, which ended Captain Roberts's landing business. Shipping by rail using refrigerator cars for produce became the standard method of transportation. The railroad also allowed for people to travel a long distance in a short time. The California Packing Corporation, Del Monte Plant Nine, was located by the San Lorenzo Railroad Station to ship the products and provide seasonal work for the town. San Lorenzo was known as the largest producer of farm crops in California.

By 1860, the town's population expanded with the arrival of immigrants from Portugal, Italy, Spain, Denmark, Ireland, and other countries. With the completion of the Transcontinental Railroad in 1869, the Chinese laborers who helped build it came to work on the farms. In the 1900s, Japanese immigrants began to arrive, most in the nursery business, growing flowers and specialty crops such as strawberries. Today many descendents of these immigrants still live in the San Lorenzo area.

The first building boom came to the Bay Area in the 1920s. Ashland, Hayward Acres, and Cherryland were subdivided, and new homes were built. Fruit, vegetables, poultry, and farm animals were raised on small farms. The greatest building boom was the development of homes during World War II, located south of the San Lorenzo Creek, which turned the farmland into a suburban community. The developer, David D. Bohannon, became a celebrity within the property-development community for his method of building the houses and his planned community, including a homeowner's association.

The town of San Lorenzo was changing. With the increased population, the library and post office moved to larger facilities in the San Lorenzo Village. The sudden growth left the San Lorenzo School District so short on space that students were being taught in empty houses and a church. There were split sessions and double sessions at the established schools. A school building program rapidly began. Houses and businesses were moved or demolished for freeways. Roads were widened and land was annexed by the surrounding cities.

The steady population growth brought more churches, recreation areas, service groups, and programs for the community. Currently the Alameda County Redevelopment Agency, working with three Citizens Advisory Committees, is planning the future of this unincorporated area of Eden Township in Alameda County.

One

OLD SAN LORENZO

Native Americans called Ohlone originally inhabited the area now known as San Lorenzo. The Spanish called them *Costanoan*, which means "coastal people" in Spanish. They lived along San Lorenzo Creek and near the present-day Fairmont Hospital area, where water was available from a spring. These native people found that the fertile land made for an excellent living location.

Spanish padres and soldiers, on expeditions looking for mission sites, left journals of their findings. They saw native villages along the creek, called El Arroyo San Lorenzo, which was later changed to San Lorenzo Creek. There was lush vegetation and an abundance of game. Many tracks of elk, deer, coyote, mountain lion, grizzly bear, and other animals were seen. Wild flowers covered the area, and willow, sycamore, and oak trees lined the creek. Wild fowl filled the bay lands and marshes.

The San Lorenzo area that the Spanish soldiers had explored and mapped in 1769 would become the grazing lands of Mission San Jose in 1797. In 1821, Mexico declared its independence from Spain and took possession of California and the missions. The land was granted as ranchos to soldiers and politicians. Don Jose Joaquin Estudillo, in 1842, received Rancho San Leandro from the Mexican government. Rancho San Lorenzo was granted to Guillermo Castro. It included present-day Castro Valley, Hayward, and part of San Lorenzo. Castro's daughter Barbara Soto and son-in-law Francisco were granted the lower section of San Lorenzo. America won California from Mexico in 1848, and it became a state in 1850.

The gold rush brought men to California who found more value in the rich farmlands of San Lorenzo than in the soil of the Sierra. The beauty of the area, the mild climate, and the fertile soil were like magnets. So many squatters resided along the banks on the north side of San Lorenzo Creek that their settlement was known as Squatterville from 1847 until 1854 when it became San Lorenzo. The town became known as an important shipping area, a prosperous farm community with many mansions, and a resort spot for visitors.

OFFICIAL ATLAS MAP, 1878. This map of the first San Lorenzo town layout is in Thompson and West's *New Historical Atlas of Alameda County*. Note the property owners and the location of the cemetery, church, and school. The dotted lines show the driveways to the mansions of C. W. Hathaway and William Meek. The first business opened in 1853, located on the south side of San Lorenzo Creek, known as the PlowShop or blacksmith shop of John Boyle. Upon his death, Henry Smith, his employee, bought the business. Only College and Sycamore Streets names remained, as the others have been changed; Robert's Landing Road and Main Street are now Lewelling Boulevard, Adams Street is now Albion Avenue, Telegraph Road is Hesperian Boulevard, Walnut Street was eliminated, Second Street is now Usher Street, Third Street is Tracy Street, Fourth Street is Ronda Street, Fifth Street is Via Granada, and Sixth Street is now a private road to duplexes. The author's great-grandparents purchased a house and property in 1875 at the corner of Main and Fourth Streets in block 17.

JACOB WRIGHT HARLAN. The leader of the squatters was Jacob Harlan, a scout with General Fremont. In his book, *California '46 to '88*, he reminiscences about the founding of Squatterville, later called San Lorenzo. He organized some farmers and formed an association for the taking up of claims on sections of land.

SAN LORENZO'S FIRST HOTEL. The San Lorenzo House was opened in 1853 by Albert E. Crane at the northeast corner of what is now Hesperian and Lewelling Boulevards. In 1864, it became the first post office for San Lorenzo, with Crane as the postmaster. James Frandsen later purchased the building and operated the hotel and tavern for more than 50 years. In the 1960s, the hotel was demolished to widen Hesperian Boulevard.

ROBERT'S LANDING AND RESIDENCE. The above 1853 illustration of Robert's Landing from Thompson and West's *New Historical Atlas of Alameda County* shows a long wharf and several warehouses. It was the link for local farmers to ship grain, fruits, vegetables, and lumber products from the redwood groves of Castro Valley to San Francisco. Located at the mouth of San Lorenzo Creek and the end of current Lewelling Boulevard, it was also a receiving point for the town. William Roberts also operated a freight and passenger schooner, known as the *Helen Eliza*, and a lumber business. He owned 450 acres of marshland and farmland in the current Washington Manor area. In 1869, he built his family home near the "Four Corners." Seen in the 1999 photograph below, Captain Roberts's house, located west of the freeway underpass on Lewelling Boulevard, is now privately owned.

SAN LORENZO FARMER. This is an 1879 illustrated portrait of Leonard Stone, who came to San Lorenzo in 1853 at age 27 from Massachusetts. He purchased 123 acres and was a charter officer of the San Lorenzo Pioneer Cemetery Association with John Marlin, Henry Smyth, and G. Knapp. He died in 1888 and is buried with his wife, Jane, and two children under two years old, at the Pioneer Cemetery.

CRANE FAMILY RESIDENCE. Albert Crane opened the first hotel and tavern in 1853, located at the northeast corner of Main Street and Telegraph Road, named for the telegraph poles erected along the road. Later the street became Hesperian Boulevard. The house was located on Crane's pear orchard on the northwest side of Hesperian Boulevard. It burned in 1912.

LEWELLING FAMILY MANSION. The 1878 *New Historical Atlas of Alameda County* by Thompson and West illustrates the Lewelling family home. Henderson Lewelling came from Oregon with William Meek and purchased 120 acres of land in the area of Main and East Fourteenth Streets. Son John and grandson Eli also bought land to extend their horticultural businesses. After the death of Eli, Main Street was renamed Lewelling Boulevard.

MEEK FAMILY MONUMENT. Located in the San Lorenzo Pioneer Cemetery is the elaborate Meek plot. John Lewelling and William Meek owned the three-acre cemetery land at the corner of College Street and Hesperian Boulevard. On March 19, 1864, the San Lorenzo Cemetery Association purchased the property for $500. Plots cost from $20 to $30, depending upon size and location. The cemetery is now owned and maintained by Alameda County.

MEEK MANSION AND CARRIAGE HOUSE. A gardener (above) working in the front of the elaborate 1869 mansion was one of 16 permanent employees. The house entrance faced the San Lorenzo Creek so William Meek could cross a wooden bridge to visit his horticulturist friend Henderson Lewelling's residence and the 120-acre fruit farm by current East Lewelling Boulevard. Now the property entrance is off of Meekland Avenue at the corner of Hampton and Boston Roads (below). The carriage house held not only carriages but also had stalls for horses. Horry Meek, eldest son of William, hired a full-time coachman to groom and harness the six mares for their three buggies. Today the Hayward Area Recreation and Park District owns the mansion and carriage house on 10 acres. The Hayward Area Historical Society maintains it for a future museum.

MEEK FAMILY, 1890S. William Meek Jr. (left) with wife, Carolyn Stevens Meek (center, child in lap), join Horry Meek (center) and his wife, Harriet Webb Meek (seated at far right), on the porch of the family mansion. The other ladies and children are unidentified. After William Meek's death, Horry and William Jr. managed the vast acreage of orchards and produced crops until the land was subdivided into five tracts and sold.

POST OFFICE STAFF, 1944. Three volunteers and two postal workers stand outside the Lewelling Boulevard post office. Pictured, from left to right, are unidentified, Doris Silva, unidentified, Gertrude Mooney, and Mary Videll. San Lorenzo community women volunteered to sort the mail while the villagers stood in long lines waiting to pick up it up. There was no home delivery until the post office was reclassified.

HIGH RIDE PLOW, 1875. This image was printed from an original hand-carved wood block. The high ride plow was invented and manufactured by Henry Smyth of San Lorenzo at his blacksmith shop. It was used to plow heavy adobe soil for sugar beets. One of the plows is now in the Smithsonian in Washington, D.C.

HIGH RIDE PLOW
Invented & Manufactured
By
Henry Smyth
San Lorenzo, California
CIRCA 1875

(Printed from original hand carved wood block.)

SAN LORENZO BLACKSMITH SHOP. Standing by the dapple gray team of horses is William Z. Smith, who rented the H. Smyth Blacksmith Shop until 1930 when a pipeline was laid along Hesperian Boulevard to bring water from Oakland. Sitting on the water wagon, used to keep the roads wet in summer, is John Joseph. Note the farm equipment in the front of the shop. The signs on the building advertise the Vulcanizing Company and Diamond Tires.

MAKING A WAGON WHEEL, 1905. William Z. Smith and Stuart Donaldson stand in front of the wagon area at Henry Smyth's blacksmith shop. In the foreground is a tank for setting wagon tires. The red-hot tire, having been expanded by the tire-setting press, is big enough to fit over the wagon wheel and is hammered onto the wheel. Then the tire and platform are dropped into the tank of water by means of a lever. The tire shrinks tightly on the wheel.

BLACKSMITH AND WHEELWRIGHT SHOP, 1918. Standing in the interior of the shop are proprietors Henry Braumiller (left) and William Z. Smith. They employed 30 to 40 people to make plows and wagons, shod horses, and repair farm equipment and buggies. At top right of the photograph is a price list for shoeing horses, listing the cost at $2.00 and $2.50 and resets for $1.50.

LAST BLACKSMITH SHOP. Still on Albion Avenue, formerly Adams Street, the last blacksmith shop of William Smith has been remodeled by various businesses. William Smith rented the H. Smyth Blacksmith Shop, also known as the Alameda County Agricultural Works, on Hesperian Boulevard. In 1930, he bought the blacksmith equipment, because the building was demolished for a pumping station, and established this shop on Adams Street. It was sold in 1951.

SAN LORENZO RHUBARB. This is an image of a packing label being put on strawberry rhubarb boxes at the packing sheds, which are in the background. The railroad by the shipping station at Washington Avenue and Halcyon Drive transported the fruit to the East Coast markets. San Lorenzo's climate and soil were excellent conditions for strawberry rhubarb. The Central California Rhubarb Growers' Association members shipped from the San Lorenzo Station.

19

READY TO HITCH UP THE HORSES. This spring wagon at the rear of the H. Smyth Blacksmith Shop on the San Lorenzo Creek and Telegraph Road, now Hesperian Boulevard, is ready for its owner. The office building's sign reads, "No shop tools or implements loaned."

SAN LORENZO RAILROAD STATION. In 1878, the Southern Pacific Railway Company began service from Santa Cruz to Oakland, passing through San Lorenzo at the station by the pioneer cemetery on what is now Hesperian Boulevard. Southern Pacific Railroad bought the railway in 1886 and transported not only freight but also had passenger trains during the day.

SAN LORENZO STREET SCENE, 1890S. A horse-drawn trolley coach travels down Telegraph Road, now Hesperian Boulevard, toward the Willows Hotel that was built by the San Lorenzo Creek Bank in 1875. People from San Francisco liked the country air and would stay at the hotel. They also bought farm products and visited San Lorenzo Grove, a recreation park, and the Village Hall.

VILLAGE HALL, 1901. The San Lorenzo Fruit Processing Company built the hall in 1864, on the corner of now Lewelling Boulevard and Usher Street, to use as a warehouse for drying fruit. In 1891, the Village Hall Association formed and purchased the building for the town's social center and first library. In 1924, Jack Marlin bought the building for his machine shop until he relocated, and in 1954, the hall was demolished.

SAN LORENZO PAVILION. A trolley company owned this building, facing current Tracy Street, and eight-acre natural park called San Lorenzo Grove from 1895 to 1911. Manuel S. Rodgers purchased the property and made it an amusement park for 10 years. He replaced the aging trees with an apricot orchard and used the pavilion's lumber to build the corner house on Tracy Street and Lewelling Boulevard in the 1920s.

RURAL LETTER CARRIER. Joe Correa, the first rural letter carrier for the San Lorenzo Post Office, served from June 1, 1904, until June 30, 1924. He delivered mail in a 30-mile area with a two-wheeled Studebaker buggy drawn by his horse, Babe. His daughter Bernice Thomas lives close to her grandfather Frank Correa's restored house on Hesperian Boulevard, beyond Halcyon Drive.

SHIMAN'S GENERAL STORE.
Located on what is now Hesperian
Boulevard and Albion Street by
the San Lorenzo Creek was John
L. Shiman's store. It had a variety
of merchandise, from fabric and
groceries to seeds and farm supplies.
Mail was delivered by horseback to
the post office in the store with John
Shiman as postmaster from 1859 to
1893. Grandson Jack Shiman had a
flower shop on Lewelling Boulevard
in the 1950s.

SAN LORENZO'S OLDEST CHURCH.
Dedicated on July 4, 1875, at the
corner of College and Usher Streets,
the Christian Union Society
Church stood until it closed during
the 1930s Depression. With the
establishment of the San Lorenzo
Village, it was reopened in 1944.
Soon the congregation built a larger
church on Paseo Grande, and in
1949, sold the church to the First
Southern Baptist congregation.

WILLOWS HOTEL AND EMBERS. The second hotel in San Lorenzo, built in 1875 by Ezra Livingston, was across the San Lorenzo Creek from the H. Smyth Blacksmith Shop facing Telegraph Road, now Hesperian Boulevard. It was the gathering place for local residents and visitors who vacationed in the country. During the 1940s, the bottom section became the Embers Restaurant, famous for steak dinners and weekend music. With the widening of Hesperian Boulevard and an addition to the freeway, it was demolished in the 1960s. The short road that continues from the 880 Freeway off-ramp, across Lewelling Boulevard to Hesperian Boulevard in front of a modern hotel, is called Embers Way—a reminder of the old restaurant.

TRAIN BRIDGE, 1912. The Southern Pacific railroad bridge crossed over the San Lorenzo Creek by current San Lorenzo High School. On weekends, special trainloads of passengers would leave the train where it crossed current Lewelling Boulevard to walk three blocks to San Lorenzo Grove and gate of the pavilion. Along the banks of the creek people would picnic and fish.

SMYTH FAMILY PICTURE, 1946. A descendent of the Smyth family, Russell Smyth, identified his family members, from left to right, as (first row) Russell's mother Jone Westover Smyth, Russell's grandmother Johanna Fitter Smyth, Lillie Smyth, and Florence Buck; (second row) Thomas Buck, Elsie Smyth Dennis, Jim Dennis, Mary Smyth, Russell's grandfather Harry T. Smyth, Laura Alice Smyth, Russell's father Harry J. Smyth, Helen Buck, and Ned Smith.

A Marlin House. In 1849, John Marlin came from Pennsylvania to the West Coast with his three brothers, Henry, Brady, and Washington. In 1852, John returned to Pennsylvania to bring his wife and family. They lived as squatters in the San Lorenzo area until Henry began purchasing his three ranches that eventually totaled 450 acres. Today original Marlin family homes still stand on Peach Drive and Lewelling Boulevard in San Lorenzo.

San Lorenzo Baptist Church, 1946. The first church was on the original property of the Moet family, where tomatoes were raised and chicken houses were located by the San Lorenzo Creek. It was built on the far south side of Lewelling Boulevard and Ronda Street. When it became too small for the congregation, a two-story building and church was built in 1955. The original church is now a meeting hall.

SAN LORENZO CATHOLIC CHURCHES. Mother of Claude Silva, Mary Ellen Faria Silva (above) stands with her bicycle by the donors of the church land, Mr. and Mrs. Enos Stanton, in 1902. In the buggy is Mr. Sampson, the carpenter. Built in 1897 and dedicated in 1901 as a mission church on what is now East Lewelling Boulevard, it was staffed by visiting priests from San Leandro. Local families took care of St. John's Catholic Church before it became a parish church in 1925 when a rectory was built. Fr. Abel Costa became the first resident priest. After World War II, the parish population exploded and the larger church (below) was built in 1950. By 1972, after serving as the parish hall, the deteriorating 75-year-old church was demolished for a parking lot, and a new gym-hall complex was completed.

STAINED GLASS WINDOW. Dedicated in memory of Albert E. Crane, the first postmaster of San Lorenzo and owner of the San Lorenzo House Hotel, the first stained glass window resides in the First Southern Baptist Church, which faces Usher Street. In 1989, Renee DeBois, a member of the church, made and hung the second stained glass window behind the baptismal, and now all the windows are stained glass.

SAN LORENZO NEIGHBORS, 1928. John Joseph, the author's grandfather, standing in front of his barn on Fourth Street, now Ronda Street, is visiting with neighbor Jim Moet while his horse is resting. Joseph was born in the old wooden house on the property. Moet's two-story wooden house is located next to the San Lorenzo Baptist Church meeting hall. Both houses are visible today.

MAIN STREET HOUSE, 1920. Mrs. Borba stands on the porch of her Lewelling Boulevard and Fifth Street home. When the San Lorenzo Village houses were built south of the creek, no bridge existed in this area. Fifth Street continued across the creek and is now called Via Granada. The Borba family lived next to the Moets.

THE SAN LORENZO GROVE HOUSE. Currently on Tracy and Sycamore Streets, this house has been occupied by many families over the years, including the caretaker of San Lorenzo Grove, Mr. Cunha. Manuel Rodgers purchased San Lorenzo Grove in 1911 and ceased operation of the park in 1920, tearing down all buildings except the caretaker's house. It became the residence of daughter Mary Videll and her husband, Frank, until their house was completed on Tracy Street.

SAN LORENZO JAPANESE CHRISTIAN CHURCH. Sunday school classes stand in front of the San Lorenzo Holiness Church, formerly located on Lewelling Boulevard near Washington Avenue, which was demolished in 1962. Kumaichiro Shinido began a nursery in Oakland before purchasing San Lorenzo property in the name of his American son, Joseph Shinido, who graduated from the San Lorenzo Grammar School. In 1929, Kumaichiro Shinido donated an acre of land and the farmhouse adjacent to his nursery for the church. It closed during World War II when the Japanese were evacuated from the West Coast and placed in internment camps. In 1944, Shinido died in such a camp. In 1949, the four Shinido sons and other volunteers built the current San Lorenzo Japanese Christian Church fronting Lewelling Boulevard. Its postal address is in San Leandro due to the 1950s annexation.

SAN LORENZO HOLINESS CHURCH, 1929. Bishop Juji Nakada, wearing the clerical collar, came from the Japan Oriental Missionary Society Holiness Conference of Japan for the dedication of this church building. Robert Shinido (at center, left of the bishop), age eight, sits by his grandfather Kumaichiro Shinido, who donated the church land and the farmhouse. The parishioners were mostly people working at the nursery.

TEUBERT HOUSE, 1884. Several unidentified people stand looking out at Adams Street, now Albion Avenue, which is parallel to Lewelling Boulevard by the San Lorenzo Creek. This house was built by Herman Teubert in 1864 and had 13 rooms, including seven bedrooms and one bathroom. William Z. Smith rented a room while working at Smyth's blacksmith shop and married Frederica Teubert. They had one son, William Teubert Smith.

BOWERS HOUSE, 1895. A small boy sits on the front porch of the Bower family home, looking out across the country road of Main Street, now Lewelling Boulevard. Later the house was sold to the Poston family, and it burned down in the 1960s. A supply warehouse is now on the property.

OLD TANK HOUSE. Mary Rodgers Videll stands with her father, Manuel Rodgers, by the family home and farm in the area stretching from the entrance of current Lewelling Boulevard to Mattox Road. Arriving from the Azores Islands in 1876 at 19 years old, Manuel worked for Eli Lewelling as a foreman. Later he purchased the 58 acres of land bordering East Fourteenth Street. Today Bancheros Restaurant is located on part of the property.

LAST BARN AND FARM. The last farm (above) in San Lorenzo was originally bought by Herman Nielson and Theodore Bagge, immigrants from Denmark, in 1870. Herman bought Theodore's share in 1875. On the remaining 200 acres, he built a barn and house on the section south of the San Lorenzo Creek on Washington Avenue. After his death, his wife and three sons subdivided the property into small sections. In 1929, the Ferro, Ronconi, Lagomarsino, and Croce families bought the barn-area section of the property. When the vegetable farming ended, Ferro and Ronconi sold the farm for homes in 1998. The gasoline tank and all equipment (below) were sold, but some of the barn boards were saved. The barn is now known as the Nielson-Ferro Barn.

VIERRA HOUSE, 1945. Daisy the dog stands by rows of asparagus along the Washington Avenue home of Antone and Caroline Vierra. A fishpond is in the front yard. The house and family moved behind Frank Sobrero's Gasoline Station on Lewelling Boulevard when the freeway and Washington Avenue overpass were built. They lived there until their San Lorenzo Village home was completed on land Antone and brother George had farmed.

HYGELUND HOUSE, 1945. Located next to the Vierra House was the Hygeland family home and farm. A fence with a gate, which allowed the friends easy access to each other's property, separated the two farms. Other neighbors included the Salel's, who had a grocery store and gas station on the corner of Lewelling Boulevard and Washington Avenue; the Perry Ranch; and the Freitas's secondhand auto-parts warehouse.

VIERRA'S LONG DRIVEWAY. Caroline carries in the milk bottles that were delivered at the fence near the edge of Box 35 Washington Avenue. Across the street lived the Nicolotti family, with 10 acres and a huge stand. The Nicolottis sold chickens, rabbits, flowers, fruit, vegetables, and chicken eggs. They also took their farm products to the local Piggly Wiggly stores.

VIERRA COUSINS, 1935. In the backyard of the Vierra's Washington Avenue home and 10 acre farm stands Shirley, who is visiting her cousin Tom. At right is the tank house that all farms used to store their water. Shirley and Tom's fathers were farming partners and grew tomatoes in San Lorenzo.

LAUREL OR BAY TREE, 1900.
Along Main Street, now East Lewelling Boulevard, this tree still stands across from San Lorenzo High School. William Meek purchased four acres on the south and four acres on the north side of the San Lorenzo Creek for his sister, Mrs. Teel, who moved from Oregon with three children when her husband died.

FAMOUS SAN LORENZO TREE. This tree is located across from San Lorenzo High School on the former Teel property. It is the world's largest laurel, or bay tree, according to University of California authorities in a Hayward newspaper article of August 8, 1945. Another feature, stated by Mary Teel, William Meek's niece, is that the ashes of her mother and sister were deposited in an aperture of the tree trunk around 1926.

FOUR CORNERS TOMATO FIELD, 1953. William Marciel, the author's father, raised beefsteak tomatoes on the Twin Nursery land at the northwest corner in San Lorenzo, behind Mac's Produce and Meat Market. The boxes were transported by the 1950s Chevrolet truck to Dennison Cannery located in Fruitvale. Now the Lewelling and Hesperian Boulevard land is in the city of San Leandro and houses business establishments.

WORKING THE LAND, 1946. At the corner of Lewelling Boulevard and Third Street, now Tracy Street, William Marciel and his eight-year-old daughter, Doris, use a "drag" behind the horses to smooth the land for growing tomatoes. The O'Connor sisters owned the land and boardinghouse at the corner of Second Street, now Usher Street and Lewelling Boulevard.

STENZEL PROPERTY, 1932. George Vierra, wife Isabel, and daughter Shirley lived in this house where the Hayward Airport is now located. From 1932 to 1939, George and brother Antone rented 250 acres from the Stenzel Estate Company, Inc. The brothers grew corn, rhubarb, hay, and tomatoes. They jointly owned four acres of choice land, purchased from J. P. Marlin, off of current Paseo Grande.

MONTGOMERY HOUSE, 2000. This house, built in the early 1900s, is located on the corner of Usher and Sycamore Streets. It is one of two historical houses on Usher Street, the other being the Jorgensen house down the street. This area was the center of the first town of San Lorenzo, which incorporated the first church, school, library, post office, and recreation area.

JOSEPH FAMILY, 1930S. The Joseph family lived at Lewelling Boulevard and Sixth Street, a dirt road ending at the San Lorenzo Creek. Charlie, standing behind a car with the family dog (above), graduated from San Lorenzo Elementary School where he played in the band. He later played drums in another band, performing at Pland's Villa Restaurant, the Alabam' Club, Our House, and the Embers Restaurant. Brother Joseph F. Joseph, standing by his car at the family home (below) and also a graduate of San Lorenzo Elementary School, was in World War II. His name is inscribed on the San Lorenzo All Wars Memorial. The family also stabled palomino horses on their property to ride in parades. Their father, Joseph P. Joseph Jr., was a trustee for the San Lorenzo School District in the 1940s and on the Oro Loma Board of Directors from 1948 to 1952.

SILVA FAMILY HOUSE. Pictured here are Lorraine Faria (left), a cousin of the Silvas, and brothers Julian and Claude (by the bicycle) looking at two adults (note the shadows). The house was located on the rectory side of St. Johns Catholic Church. The Silva, Stanton, and Faria families were related and owned all of the frontage property on the north side of Lewelling Boulevard, from the railroad tracks to current Bar Avenue.

TOM SILVA'S TRUCKS. Pictured are two trucks owned by Tom Silva of San Lorenzo with unidentified drivers standing on trucks. The first one is a Bulldog Mack Truck that has Tom's name below a symbol on the front. It had solid tires, a chain drive, and traveled 18 miles per hour. The radiator was below the windshield. In the 1920s, Tom Silva's drayage business hauled boxes and many other materials.

THE ADAPTIVE WAGON. Tom Silva, Claude Silva's father, on his 12-acre ranch in the area of Lewelling Boulevard and Ashland Avenue, transports materials to make boxes. The wagon had a motor, steering wheel, and pedals. Instead of a horse and wagon and before the truck, this motorized wagon was used.

JACK SMITH, 1910s. Jack Smith, a San Lorenzo native, stands by his car in his apricot orchard. This property, fronting Ashland Avenue and Lewelling Boulevard, was purchased by the Hayward Union High School District for San Lorenzo High School. The Smith house was moved to face Ashland Avenue and was used for a parent cooperative nursery. A house built for his daughter, Olive Smith Silva, remains by the school facing Lewelling Boulevard.

JOSEPH JOSEPH'S HOUSE. In 1875, the author's great-grandparents purchased property on Main Street, now Lewelling Boulevard, across from the San Lorenzo Grove. Their youngest child, John, was born in the house in 1877. John met his wife, Annie, a Castro Valley native, at the San Lorenzo Grove Pavilion. Their daughter Pauline was born in 1906 in the house that still remains on the family property.

FRIENDS ON SIXTH STREET. Pictured here, from left to right, are Lolo Joseph Carson, Alice Lawson, Lawrence Carson, and MaryAnn Joseph Nunes at the Lawson house on Sixth Street off Lewelling Boulevard. Three families, the Josephs, Dennisons, and Lawsons, lived on this small street, which ended at the San Lorenzo Creek. Now the road is a private driveway for apartments.

VIDELL HOUSE, 1925. At the current corner of Tracy Street and Lewelling Boulevard, this house was built from the demolished pavilion of the San Lorenzo Grove. Mary Videll's father, Manuel Rodgers, purchased San Lorenzo Grove, an amusement park, in 1911. He operated it with his family until 1920. The recreation area was where Mary met her husband, Frank, who built the house.

CANNERY IN SAN LORENZO. The California Packing Corporation operated Del Monte Plant Nine across the street from the railroad station on Hesperian Boulevard, where the townhouses are located. A September 10, 1919, issue of *The Lug Box* stated that Plant Nine was packing peaches, pears, and tomatoes. The cannery had a nursery and playground for the employees' children.

SAN LORENZO CANNERY WORKERS. The California Packing Company operated Del Monte Plant Nine on the west side of current Hesperian Boulevard by the railroad. It provided seasonal work for the community. Pictured here, from left to right, are Mary Smith and Louise Fatado of Ashland Avenue, Annie Joseph of Lewelling Boulevard, and Carry Fatado of Ashland Avenue. They are taking a break from cannery work in the shade.

FRED'S FLOWER SHOP, 1942. Fred and Lucille Kraus stand in their first shop on Hesperian Boulevard by the San Lorenzo Creek. In 1941, they purchased Harry Imosa's Flower Shop. Nine years later, the building was demolished for the 880 Freeway exit to San Lorenzo. Their second location was across from Airport Park, now Kennedy Park, on Hesperian Boulevard. Their son Richard continues the family business at the third building on Hesperian Boulevard.

POSTON FAMILY, 1922. Sitting on the porch of their San Lorenzo home at 614 Lewelling Boulevard (above), from left to right, are (first row) Selma, Evelyn, Ruth, and Sarah Jane; (second row) Willard "Bill" Poston, mother Della, Lucille, and John. The family of five sisters and two brothers lived with their mother, who was also born in San Lorenzo and attended San Lorenzo Grammar School. Mr. Poston, the San Lorenzo School custodian, died when Evelyn was six years old. Below, Evelyn's picture was taken at her retirement in 1978; she was the San Lorenzo School District school secretary for 46 years and worked for Superintendents Clyde Lawson, Paul Ehret, and William Dolph. Miss Poston saved many artifacts from the early San Lorenzo Grammar School, which were displayed in the former San Lorenzo Schools Museum.

SAN LORENZO PIONEER CEMETERY, 1986. With the help of a parent, two Bay School fifth graders on a field trip are making tombstone rubbings of the Anna Moore monument. Not only were names inscribed on the monument, but in olden days it included the exact age of the deceased at death (such as six years, two months, one day, and the year they died), the place of birth, and other information.

SAN LORENZO CEMETERY MEETING, 1998. Planning the future of the cemetery, from left to right, are unidentified, Eileen Dalton from Alameda County Community Redevelopment Division, Barbara Debarger from San Lorenzo Unified School District, Rev. Charles Luffingwell from the First Southern Baptist Church, Alameda County supervisor Gale Steele, Maria Palmeri from Alameda County Public Works, and Alameda County grounds supervisor Dennis Nunes. One result of the meeting was the replacement of the fence.

STONE FAMILY MONUMENT, 1970S. At the San Lorenzo Pioneer Cemetery, Mr. Stone stands by one of his family monuments, located near the Meek family plot. William Meek's first wife died. His second wife, Sarah Stone, also died, and when his third wife, Mary Lewelling, died, he married Fidelia Stone, the sister of Sarah. Her name is on the Meek-Stevens-Stone monument along with her husband and her parents.

SAN LORENZO NATIVES. In July 2000, Ignatius "Nish" Rodrigues (left) received a certificate for being the oldest and longest-participating parishioner at St. Johns Catholic Church from Fr. Bill Dunn. Born in San Lorenzo in 1906, Rodrigues currently lives with his wife, Lorraine, on Ashland Avenue. Next door lives his sister Violet Wade, who was born in 1910. Both are graduates of San Lorenzo Grammar School.

MABEL BUSKEY MILLER. A native San Lorenzan, Mabel is the longest-participating member of the First Southern Baptist Church, the oldest church building in San Lorenzo, which fronts Usher Street. Her home was at Box 93 Robert's Landing Road, now Lewelling Boulevard. In 1937, the house was moved up the road where she now lives. She graduated from San Lorenzo Grammar School in 1927.

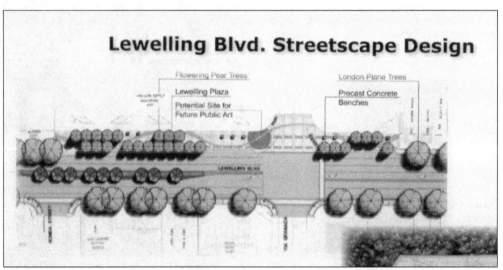

LEWELLING BOULEVARD IMPROVEMENTS. This planned streetscape design shows a new plaza section from Ronda Street to Via Granada across from the San Lorenzo Baptist Church. It will include precast concrete block benches with historical imprints of San Lorenzo history facts, landscaping, and a potential site for public art. The street will have four lanes, a landscaped median, two bicycle paths, and tree-lined sidewalks.

SAN LORENZO LIBRARIES. The first official branch of the Alameda County library system was established on November 25, 1910, in Village Hall at the current corner of Lewelling Boulevard and Usher Street. It consisted of two bookcases containing 100 books. Mary Brommage, whose house still remains on Lewelling Boulevard, was the first library custodian. Around 1925, the branch moved to an old wooden store on Hesperian Boulevard (above) close to Sycamore Street. With the establishment of the San Lorenzo Village, the branch relocated next to the firehouse on Paseo Grande in 1951. When it outgrew that building in 1969, it relocated to where the current library stands. The old library (below), purchased for $1, was moved to Via Toledo and Hacienda Avenue and currently is used as a church hall.

GONZALES'S FIRST HOME, 1950. After being discharged from the navy, Hank Gonzales purchased a Quonset hut (a trademark of semicylindrical-shaped huts) from Camp Parks in Pleasanton. Dividing the inside into rooms, his family lived there while he built the house at the back of the property that fronts current East Lewelling Boulevard. Later he removed the Quonset hut.

GONZALES FAMILY PROPERTY. Mary and Hank's property, across from St. Johns Catholic Church, borders the San Lorenzo Creek. Originally the property line was approximately 22 feet from the back of the house. Over the years, the creek bank changed during flooding and reconstruction by the Flood Control District, which was established after the big flood of December 1955. Now the creek is lined with concrete from top to bottom to avoid flooding.

EAST LEWELLING RESTAURANT, 1951. Hank Gonzales, a contractor, built this coffee shop at the front of his property on Lewelling Boulevard. It had a takeout window and was popular with San Lorenzo High School students. Later he built another business to the left of the coffee shop. The future of the restaurant and beauty parlor now depend upon the widening of East Lewelling Boulevard, with a four-lane road and median, bicycle paths, and sidewalks.

GERTRUDE V. MOONEY, 1945. Mooney, the 13th postmaster of San Lorenzo, served from 1942 to 1963, and traveled to Washington, D.C., to reclassify the "rural-free-delivery" carrier and one-clerk post office to a three-clerk and three-mail-carrier post office. Being successful, the small post office on Lewelling Boulevard, at Usher Street, moved to a village shopping center storefront on Paseo Grande in 1946.

SAN LORENZO POST OFFICE. Standing in line, the residents of San Lorenzo Village wait to receive their mail and buy stamps from the two-employee post office on Lewelling Boulevard. No mail was delivered to the village in 1944 until the post office was reclassified. It moved into the storefront at Paseo Grande in San Lorenzo Village on September 3, 1946.

SAN LORENZO'S DURANTE MARKET, 1940s. Mr. and Mrs. Durante, proprietors of Durante's Market, stand outside their grocery store at 572 Hesperian Boulevard between Adams Street, currently Albion Avenue, and Lewelling Boulevard. Mr. Durante used a ledger to record transactions when patrons wanted to charge groceries and received payment when the customer could pay the bill. Along with the San Lorenzo Village merchants, he participated in the food drives during the holiday season.

Two

SAN LORENZO VILLAGE

World War II brought thousands of people to the Bay Area to work in the many shipyards and other war-developed industries. The critical home shortage brought David D. Bohannon, a master builder, to San Lorenzo. In 1941, all home building outside of war-production centers stopped, thus ending his Hillsdale development. With the urgent need for war housing, Bohannon began constructing small housing developments. Seeking a large acreage close to the Bay Area, he found San Lorenzo. Quickly he bought Henry Smyth's large farm, and smaller farms, south of the San Lorenzo Creek.

On May 16, 1944, a year and four months before the war ended, ground was broken on the property Bohannon had bought, and bulldozers cleared the land where asparagus, tomatoes, rhubarb, apricots, and other crops had grown. Bohannon's objectives were to help the urgent war-housing needs and to create an attractive and permanent modern community.

With the slogan "Every Lot a Garden Spot" and a theme of indoor/outdoor living, San Lorenzo Village arose. To overcome the wartime obstacles of materials and labor shortages, Bohannon reversed the process of making prefab houses. The building site became a huge assembly line. The men broke the manufacturing process into a series of steps for the housing models. They counted, numbered, and cut each piece of lumber to assemble into frames, rafters, and wall panels. The entire load for one house was hauled to the concrete foundation. Multiple crews raised entire blocks of houses at a time, and this was known as the "California Method." The first 1,329 houses were completed in eight months.

David D. Bohannon not only built the houses but also established a complete community, with facilities for the homeowners. Along with the planned village came the establishment of the San Lorenzo Village Homes Association in 1945. Conditions, covenants, and restrictions are maintained by an elected five-member board of directors and a salaried administrator. A yearly assessment is paid by each homeowner. Some people said it would never work, but the unincorporated community of San Lorenzo Village and its local government has lasted for more than 60 years.

McConaghy Mansion, 1800s. Neil McConaghy's second home (above) on Telegraph Road, now Hesperian Boulevard, was built by John Harr in 1886. This side view shows the house, water tank, and carriage house, which is currently owned by the Hayward Area Parks and Recreation District and operated as a museum by the Hayward Area Historical Society. John, the youngest of five children, lived in the house until his death in 1972 at age 100. He had moved there with his bride, Florence Smyth, in 1912 to take care of his parents. John's sister Mary lived in the house until her death in 1939 at age 73. Also pictured (below) is John McConaghy in 1905 with his prize team of horses and buggy in front of Hayward Hotel. The buggy was restored and is displayed in the carriage house.

FIRST MCCONAGHY HOUSE. In 1863, Neil McConaghy married Sarah McCaw and they raised five children in their first home on Grant Line Road, now Grant Avenue. The home was on the San Lorenzo Creek side by the current railroad tracks. Their neighbors across the tracks were David and Dora Snow. In 1886, the family moved to Telegraph Road, now Hesperian Boulevard.

SECOND MCCONAGHY HOUSE. Neil and Sarah McConaghy sit on the top step of their house. Below them, from left to right, are son Neal, daughter-in-law Mary, daughter Florence, and son John. John Harr, a local builder, constructed the house located on Telegraph Road. Today the Hayward Area Parks and Recreation District owns the house, and the Hayward Area Historical Society maintains it as a museum.

MARLIN WOMEN, 1900. Standing on the rails of the fence are five Marlin family women and one small boy. John and Eliza Marlin came to Squatterville, now San Lorenzo, in 1852. They farmed land by Robert's Landing and in the current San Lorenzo Village area. After their death, some of the children continued to farm and built their own homes on the land.

MARLIN RANCH, 1900. Japanese laborers are picking peas between the fruit trees in the area that is now San Lorenzo Village. Some farmers planted crops between the trees to produce more vegetables and fertilize the ground with the vines.

GRANT AVENUE HOUSE, 1944. Pictured, from left to right, are sisters Ermaline, Rosaline, Lillian (holding son Melvin Jr.), and Margaret. They are standing at the back of their parents' house where Lillian, husband Melvin, and their baby lived. Manuel and Mamie Marks, parents of the sisters, moved from Oakland to San Lorenzo in the early 1900s. The sisters attended San Lorenzo Grammar School and Hayward High School.

JOHN PETER MARLIN HOUSE, 2002. Located on Peach Drive, off Via Granada in San Lorenzo Village, is the Marlin house. John Peter's parents, John and Eliza, moved from Pennsylvania to Squatterville (later called San Lorenzo) in 1852. John Peter's son John Edward (known as Jack Marlin) was the caretaker of the San Lorenzo Cemetery. His house and property are located at Lewelling Boulevard and Usher Street.

HENRY SMYTH HOME. The Henry Smyth family is sitting on the front porch of their six-bedroom, 11-room mansion, built in 1877 by John Harr. It was first located at the corner of Grant Avenue and Hesperian Boulevard until the David D. Bohannon Organization moved it across the street. It contained a day-care center and mortuary before it was demolished in 1968 for the on-ramp to the freeway.

SMYTH FAMILY FOREMAN. Sue Woo, the "boss on Smyth Ranch," poses in his Chinese clothes. Many Chinese came to work on farms in the East Bay after leaving the gold fields. Skilled in farming, some became sharecroppers, giving a percentage of the crop to the landowner, and some rented land. Others, like Woo, became managers and foremen. The Smyth Ranch was located in the area of Hesperian Boulevard and Grant Avenue.

THE VIERRA BROTHERS. Pictured above are Antone (left) and George sorting tomatoes on their four-acre farm, purchased from J. P. Marlin, that fronts current Paseo Grande and Via Toledo in San Lorenzo Village. They picked and sorted the tomatoes to place in boxes with their stenciled brand, as seen in the image below. The pole tomatoes were transported to the Oakland market. In the *History of Alameda County Volume II*, printed in 1928, there is a biographical section on George Vierra. It states, "The Vierra brothers near San Lorenzo are numbered among Alameda County's most progressive, energetic and prosperous farmers, having showed excellent judgement in the management of their affairs." George owned five acres planted with cherries on East Fourteenth Street. Antone owned 10 acres on Washington Avenue, where he farmed and built his home.

GRANT AVENUE HOUSE AND BARN. Erik Terkelsen, originally from Denmark, built this barn (above) and house (below) on his 10-acre San Lorenzo farm with the help of neighbors. He grew vegetables and apricots. Son Fred, born in 1894 in San Francisco, helped his mother, Elizabeth, after the accidental death of his 37-year-old father, who was mysteriously shot in the stomach while working in the field in 1908. No one knew where the bullet came from. Daughter Elvira was born a few months after the death of her father. The Marks family, who lived across the street, helped the family. In 1951, the San Lorenzo Elementary School District purchased the property from the family for Grant Elementary School.

WOODWARD FAMILY, 1940s. Seated on the porch of the Terkelsen house, from left to right, are Claire, Elwyn, and Elvira Woodward, with the family dog Penny. Elvira, the daughter of Erik Terkelsen, lived on the Grant Avenue farm before it was purchased by the San Lorenzo Elementary School District to build Grant Elementary School.

SAN LORENZO FLOODS. There were various floods in the San Lorenzo area, with the last one occurring in December 1955. With heavy rains, the San Lorenzo Creek would overflow and flood parts of San Lorenzo Village, Ashland Avenue, Cherryland, Washington Manor, and other areas. The Flood Control District eliminated the problem. This photograph shows a truck on Bockman Road going to the hog farm in the 1930s.

HEIDE HOUSE, 1900S. In 1901, Henry Heide bought 10 acres of land on Grant Avenue in San Lorenzo from the estate of Herman Nielson. As a wedding gift, he built his wife, Sarah, a large farmhouse where they raised five children—Edna, Alice, Emma, John, and Fred. In 1931, Henry died, and Sarah remained in the house with Fred. The property was sold in 1989, and the house is now the Village Realtors.

HEIDE FAMILY, 1945. Emma Heide Burton, principal of San Lorenzo Elementary School, the third school located on the site at Second Street, now Usher Street, stands by the brick building. Her sister, Edna Heide Pearson, was a primary teacher at the school and the author's instructor. Emma and Edna, daughters of Henry and Sarah Heide, later lived at Fort Jones, California.

DENEVI FAMILY FIELD. Katherine Denevi stands between daughter Marie and son Frank Jr. on Bockman Road in San Lorenzo. The family raised daffodils, gladioli, and tulips, which father Frank Sr. planted, harvested, and cut for San Francisco's wholesale flower market. In 1948, a section of the 30 acres was sold to the San Lorenzo Elementary School District for Bohannon Junior High School.

FRANK DENEVI JUNIOR. On the first step of the house is Frank Jr., with his dog Rover. At 12 years old, he would see jackrabbits, pheasants, and other animals in his backyard on Bockman Road and visit the pig farm at the end of the road. During World War II, the barracks at the Hayward Airport by A Street were close to his parent's property and he watched as planes landed and departed the airport.

DENEVI MEN, 1948. Frank Jr. and Frank Sr. stand in front of their Dodge car. Frank Jr. attended Sunset Elementary School in San Lorenzo and graduated from Hayward High School in 1952. He was always interested in photography and was in charge of the photography labs in high school, at San Francisco City College, and in the army. He opened his first camera shop on his family's Bockman Road property.

LEWIS RENTS, 1946. Mr. Lewis purchased the Lewis Rents property located by the San Lorenzo Creek Bridge in 1946 and began renting tools to the new San Lorenzo Village homeowners. In 1964, Lake Lupher Jr. bought the business and property. After his death in 1982, his wife and daughters Nancy Quintel and Becky Wittmer managed the business. They expanded the rental equipment selection and have over 20 employees.

RESTING ON THE FRONT STEPS, 1952. Manuel Bulcao looks across Hesperian Boulevard where San Lorenzo Village homes were being built east of Grant Avenue. He and his daughter Mathilda, son-in-law Manuel, and granddaughter Paula Amaral moved from their 15888 Hesperian Boulevard property when the David D. Bohannon Organization purchased the land and built stores on the north side of Hesperian Boulevard.

MANUEL BULCAO'S RANCH. By 1952, Bulcao had sold 24 acres of his ranch by San Lorenzo Creek, below Washington Avenue fronting Lewelling Boulevard, for homes. One acre remained for the relocation of his Hesperian Boulevard house. Unfortunately the Hesperian Boulevard Bridge was too narrow for the house, so David D. Bohannon built a San Lorenzo Village–style house on the property.

THE HISTORY OF ORO LOMA

1911–2006

95 years of
dedicated services
to our community

To
Provide
the
Best
Possible
Service
at
the
Lowest
Possible
Cost

ORO LOMA SANITARY DISTRICT. In 1911, the Alameda County Board of Supervisors voted to approve a 29-man petition to create a new sanitary district. It would include all planned housing tracts and be called Oro Loma. A five-member board was elected and the boundaries were established. In 1917, the district became dormant due to lack of urban development, but in 1940, it reorganized and continues today at the Grant Avenue plant.

SAN LORENZO POST OFFICE. The staff of four carriers and four clerks stand in front of the fourth San Lorenzo Post Office, located at 131 Paseo Grande. Identified staff are Culver Lewis (third from left), Gertrude Mooney (fourth from left), and Mary Videll (fifth from left). It was opened on September 3, 1946, after postmaster Gertrude Mooney and the community protested against the annexation of the San Lorenzo Post Office to another station.

BOHANNON AND PLANNED COMMUNITY. An article in the April 1943 *American Builder* magazine shows David D. Bohannon next to his planned community. With his staff, he proved that private industry had the ability to do the job in the best, quickest, and most economical way in order to meet war-housing needs. At the same time, an attractive and permanent modern community was created.

BUILDING SAN LORENZO VILLAGE. Construction was organized into crews, each with a definite task to perform. Multiple crews raised entire blocks of houses at one time, and each crew had to maintain a rigid schedule to avoid blocking or slowing the operations behind them. In this photograph, workers stack and assemble the walls. It was demonstrated that the assembly-line method used fewer man-hours.

AERIAL VIEW OF THE VILLAGE. A single developer, the David D. Bohannon Organization, under wartime housing needs, acquired almost the entire area known as San Lorenzo Village. He built over 4,500 homes and set aside land for schools, churches, and shopping centers. Other developers built tracts of homes around the main development. Note the McConaghy House and Bockman Road at bottom right.

VILLAGE HOUSE EXTERIOR, 1944. Wartime limitations made it necessary to build all 1,500 houses from the same basic plan. Only variation of color and exterior finish avoided repetitive monotony. Material shortages eliminated garages, but a concrete slab was supplied, which allowed owners to erect garages later. Some used the area for sunbathing, barbecues, or parking their car.

SAN LORENZO VILLAGE. This cul-de-sac area of a village street depicts how home owners personalized their houses and gardens. Sycamore trees were provided and maintained; conditions, covenants, and restrictions were established; and a home owner association was formed. Bylaws assured home owners fire protection, clean streets, playgrounds, and a community center. A yearly assessment of $25, with automatic membership, was set.

SAN LORENZO VILLAGE SIDE DOOR. The 1944 group of Bohannon houses located in the Grant Avenue and Hesperian Boulevard area featured a bedroom with its own entrance. A war worker renting the room and working the night shift at a shipyard could enter and exit without disturbing the family. Today some side doors are covered over, and others are still in use.

SAN LORENZO VILLAGE LEGEND, 1993. At the San Lorenzo Village Homes Association Halloween party, from left to right, are association board president Carol Davis, David D. Bohannon, and association administrator Nancy Van Huffel. David D. Bohannon, the real estate legend who established San Lorenzo Village, attended the Halloween parties until his death.

SAN LORENZO VILLAGE COMMUNITY CENTER. Planning San Lorenzo Village in 1944, David D. Bohannon established a home owner association and community center complex on current Paseo Grande. It consists of the community center and office, library, firehouse, playground, and Girl Scout cabin. In 2005, the San Lorenzo Village Homes Association celebrated 60 years as one of the oldest and largest home owners associations in the country and dedicated its remodeled building.

SAN LORENZO VILLAGE FIRE DEPARTMENT. In 1948, village fire chief Tom Ducey makes a payment for the new fire engine to the Maxim Fire Equipment representative. Pictured here, from left to right, are Al LaCrone from the San Lorenzo Village Homes Association, Ducey, Ashland fire chief Lester Olivera, the Maxim Fire Equipment representative, and Cherryland fire chief Vic Hubbard.

SAN LORENZO VILLAGE MAP, 1959. The uneven boundary at left is the San Lorenzo Creek, the northern and southern borders are Southern Pacific Railroad tracks, and bordering the village at right are the Hayward Area Recreation and Park District lands, the Hayward Airport, more housing, and Hacienda Avenue. The dotted lines denote housing tracts, not members of the San Lorenzo Village Homes Association.

LORENZO THEATER, 1947. A great event took place in San Lorenzo Village when the theater opened on April 5, 1947. By invitation only, David Bohannon, all the members of the Merchants Association, and the San Lorenzo Village Homes Association were to come attired in their formal dress to see movies and attend a cocktail party at the San Lorenzo Homes Association Community Center. United Artists purchased the land on Hesperian Boulevard from the David D. Bohannon Organization and built the $465,000, 700-seat theater. The family- and community-oriented theater prospered until the 1970s when neighboring cinemas appeared and attendance declined. It was leased and sold but never succeeded. The seats were removed and the theater fell into disrepair in 1982. In 1998, the Lorenzo Theater Association formed and hopes to purchase and restore the theater as a center for visual and performing arts.

LORENZO THEATER MURALS. The murals depict black panthers prowling through exotic foliage in tropical shades of browns and greens threaded with gold. The artist, Dutch-born Anthony Heinsbergen, created the murals with fluorescent paint. When black lights are lit in the darkened theater, the murals are vivid. Heinsbergen's work was in 750 theaters nationwide, including Oakland's Paramount Theater. Less than 200 of these theaters remain today.

SAN LORENZO LITTLE LEAGUE. In May 1953, the San Lorenzo Village Homes Association Board of Directors voted to buy nine acres of land on Grant Avenue for a recreational park. They leased the property in 1958 for $1 per year to the San Lorenzo Little League. Volunteers built the diamonds, fences, and restrooms and established fields before opening day in 1959. Over the years, the rent has increased and girls now participate.

SAN LORENZO VILLAGE PARADE. A mile-long parade with bands, drill teams, scouting groups, old cars, and community organizations preceded Santa Claus on the truck, which was followed by many children. In the plaza bordered by Hesperian Boulevard, Paseo Grande, Via Arriba, and Via Mercado, Santa Claus distributed candy and trophies to the parade participants. The parade, sponsored by the Village Homes Association, also held a theater party for the children.

SANTA CLAUS VISITS. In 1946, San Lorenzo Village children rush to see Santa, standing on the back of a truck in the plaza parking lot. Behind the lot is the nearly completed Pland's Villa Restaurant and across Hesperian Boulevard is the partially constructed Lorenzo Theater. In later years, Santa Claus arrived by helicopter at the Hayward Airport and was taken by the San Lorenzo Village fire truck to the plaza.

SAN LORENZO COMMUNITY CHURCH. By 1945, the little white church at the corner of College and Usher Streets was overcrowded due to the new San Lorenzo Village homes. The congregation decided to purchase the navy seabee's McGann Chapel (above) at Camp Parks in Pleasanton and move it to the Bohannon Corporation–allocated site on Paseo Grande in 1947. The church was renamed San Lorenzo Community Church, and the congregation moved into the building in December 1948. Architect Bruce Goff designed the military basic prefab Quonset-type structure. He added salmon-red brick, redwood walls, blue glass, and acoustical tile to create a building that is architecturally acclaimed in design books today. The little white church was purchased by the First Southern Baptist Church congregation in 1949 for $15,000 and continues today. In 1974, the Community Church congregation celebrated its centennial (below).

SAN LORENZO VILLAGE STOREFRONTS. Van's Bakery was owned by San Lorenzo Village resident Kurt Van Reisin. Upon Kurt's sudden death in 1958, his wife, Eve, continued the business until 1977. It was sold to Willie Hoppe, who made it a popular European-style pastry shop and employed 13 people. It closed along with the other stores after Mervyn's Department Store moved and the David D. Bohannon Organization planned to build a new shopping area.

THE ANDREW WILLIAMS STORE. This supermarket at the corner of Hesperian Boulevard and Paseo Grande sold groceries, household items, and liquor and contained a soda fountain and Wilmart Candies. The Andrew Williams store block, which included service shops such as a shoe repair, barber shop, beauty shop, and the post office, was completed April 15, 1945. When the supermarket closed, the large store was divided into small shops.

SAN LORENZO VILLAGE PLAZA. In 1948, Pland's Villa and the Lorenzo Theater were two of the 20 establishments in the plaza. Today the art deco theater building remains empty. It was designed by Alexander Cantin, famous for his unique marquee designs. Although closed in 1982, the theater received an Art Deco Preservation Award in 1986. "San Lorenzo Village" is now written vertically on the Pland's Villa sign structure.

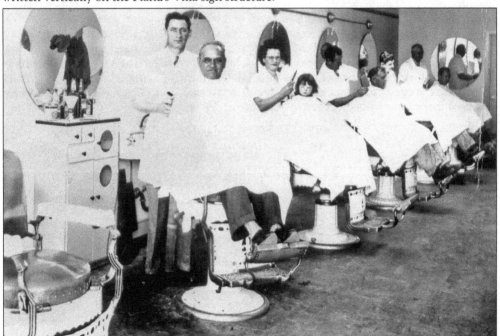

VILLAGE BARBERSHOP, 1948. The advertisement for the barbershop in the *Daily Review*'s special, "San Lorenzo Village Model Shopping Plaza Progress Edition," contained this photograph along with the following caption: "Dan Willis, the mad butcher of Paseo Grande and gang at the Village Barber Shop better known as 'The Clip Joint' say with genuine feeling WELCOME NEIGHBORS!" They were welcoming Central Bank, Peoples Drug Stores, and Village Appliance and Radio Company.

SAN LORENZO VILLAGE STOREFRONTS. Along Via Arriba was a group of stores. Pictured above, from left to right, they are Hale Hardware, Village Appliance and Radio Company, Aladdin Cleaners, Village Launderette, Hamilton Brothers Shoes, and Lorelei Children's Shop. Later a supermarket and bowling alley were added. Mervyn's, a department store seen below, opened on July 29, 1949, in the Paseo Grande storefront in the former Molen Store, next to the Village Variety. Owner Mervin Morris (the "i" was changed to a "y" by an architect) and two employees were overwhelmed with customers. In the early 1950s, Mervyn's moved to the Via Arriba storefronts (above), which were remodeled and expanded 13 times during its first 11 years. By 1976, there were 24 Mervyn's stores and more planned. Yes, Mervyn's grew up and left home, but San Lorenzo people will always remember it began in San Lorenzo Village.

GIANELLI PROPERTY, 1987. Walking along the side of the Gianelli barn on Grant and Nielson Avenues in San Lorenzo is George Gianelli's daughter Gina and their dog Misty. The Gianelli brothers, Nino and George, sold the carnation nursery land to Citation Homes in 1987. During this year, five nurseries in Alameda County were sold to developers for condominiums or shopping centers.

GIANELLI CARNATION BOUQUET, 1971. Sisto Gianelli gives carnations from his nursery at the corner of Nielson and Grant Avenues in San Lorenzo to his wife, Maria. In 1913, he came from Genoa, Italy, and Maria and two children, Nino and Irma, arrived in 1921. They established a nursery and residence where sons George and Lorenzo were born. Nino and George continued the nursery upon the death of their parents, until 1987.

ALL WARS DISPLAY, 1999. Nino Gianelli stands by the San Lorenzo Elementary School Service Roll of 93 eighth-grade graduates that served in World War II. Among the names are his brother George and many friends. The names were engraved on the San Lorenzo All Wars Memorial, rectangular granite monuments located in the garden of the Village Realtors on Grant Avenue.

ALL WARS MEMORIAL. Dedicated on June 12, 1999, the memorial consists of four large reddish, rectangular granite sections with names engraved by Bob Mattos. In the garden next to Village Realtors on Grant Avenue, the memorial honors all veterans that now live or have lived in the San Lorenzo area. Realtors Cathy and Tom Clements spearheaded the project with various organizations.

SAN LORENZO VILLAGE CELEBRATION, 2005. Frances Nelson, daughter of David D. Bohannon, rides in an antique car during the San Lorenzo Homes Association's 60th anniversary parade. A University of California at Berkeley graduate, Frances helped her father with World War II housing in San Lorenzo. Today she is a vice president of the David D. Bohannon Organization and president of the Bohannon Development Company.

THE DAVIS FAMILY. On May 6, 1955, newlyweds John and Patricia Davis visited the Brad-Rick model home on Bockman Road in San Lorenzo Village. They put down a deposit of $10 to reserve the only house left in the tract. Four months later, they moved into the bare house on Via Toyon. The total price for the house was $12,200. In 1963, their son Dan was born.

SAN LORENZO VILLAGE HOMEOWNER. Pat Davis, an original owner in the Rick-Davis tract off Channel Street, is pictured above after moving into her house in 1955. Monthly payments, including tax, insurance, and interest, were $67.98. The car in the driveway belongs to neighbor Lou Pagni, another original homeowner. The house directly across the street was still under construction, and there are no fences or lawns. Although these houses were not constructed by the David D. Bohannon Organization, they paid $25 a year to the San Lorenzo Village Homes Association. The image below shows the same location 50 years later. The two original owners, Pagni and Davis, still live in the same houses on Via Toyon.

SAN LORENZO VILLAGE FAMILY. The Halbach family moved into their house at 1417 Via Barrett on December 15, 1955. They are some of the original owners in this particular development of the village that chose not to belong to the San Lorenzo Village Homes Association. Standing in front of their house in 1973, from left to right, are (first row) Nancy and Lorilyn; (second row) Harold, Janice, and Danny.

LORENZO MANOR HOME. In 1951, Elinor and Charles Reinhart became owners of a Lorenzo Manor development house on the former Perkins farm property. The house fronted Hathaway Avenue in San Lorenzo, cost $10,850, and had three bedrooms and one bathroom. Today Elinor Reinhart-Humphrey lives on Hacienda Avenue (the street's name was changed) in the remodeled house, which now has four bedrooms, two baths, two patios, and is valued at $600,000.

SAN LORENZO VILLAGE OWNERS. Pictured, from left to right, are Elmer, Esther, Eric, and Evan Jorgensen outside their Via Arriba home. In 1954, Elmer, Esther, and baby Eric moved into their split-level home. Developers Johnson and Panitz built the first two-story houses in the San Lorenzo Village behind the McConaghy House. The homeowners became members of the San Lorenzo Village Homes Association.

VILLAGE BOARD OF DIRECTORS. Three of the five San Lorenzo Village Homes Association board members in 1980, pictured here from left to right, are president Esther Jorgensen, Luanne Sherman, and Izola Sullivan. In 1973, Esther made history as the first woman to be elected to the board of directors. Serving for 15 years, she also set a record for the longest service on the board in its 60 years.

SAN LORENZO VILLAGE STREET SIGNS.
Early Spanish and Mexican residents and
Rancho San Lorenzo probably influenced
the town's street names. The majority of the
street names include "via," meaning "way"
or "street," followed by the name of a female
or male, tree, number, or object. There are
12 female and 12 male vias. The female
vias are Annette, Carmen, Catherine,
Coralla, Frances, Harriet, Julia, Margarita,
Rosas, Sonya, Susana, and Teresa. The
males are Eduardo, Enrico, Hermana, Jose,
Lucas, Owen, Martin, Walter, San Ardo,
San Carlos, San Juan, and San Marino.
Some streets are named for people that
lived in the area, such as Nielson Avenue
for Herman Nielson, owner of 200 acres;
George Way for George Gianelli, co-owner
of the Gianelli Brothers Nursery (right);
Via Marlin for the Marlin family farms and
homes; and Bockman Road for the William
E. Bockman family.

VILLAGE SHOE REPAIR, 1948. When David D. Bohannon and the Greenwood Corporation established the shopping plaza in the San Lorenzo Village, they leased the storefronts to meet the needs of the first 9,000 residents and others in the surrounding areas. This shoe repair shop was located between Andrew Williams Super Market and the Village Jeweler along Paseo Grande. The child and men are unidentified. Other businesses and services along this strip of stores included Village Barber Shop, Village Beauty Shop, Betty's Style Shop (specializing in women's wear), Molen Stores (men's and boy's wear), Village Variety Store, and a post office. The first Mervyn's Department Store opened in 1949 when Molen's Store vacated. Another group of stores beginning at the corner of Paseo Grande and Via Arriba were Lorelei Children's Shop, Hamilton Brothers Shoes, Village Launderette, Aladdin Cleaners, Hale Hardware, Village Appliance and Radio Company, Peoples Drug Store, and Louis Super Market. At the corner of Via Arriba and Via Mercado was the Central Bank, and Pland's Villa Restaurant was located on the corner of Via Mercado and Hesperian Boulevard. To complete the plaza complex, the Lorenzo Theater faced Hesperian Boulevard. Parking for 500 cars, with no parking meters, and no city tax was used in advertising San Lorenzo Village Plaza.

Three

GREATER SAN LORENZO

The area known today as San Lorenzo is no longer the massive 8,000-plus acres of farmland once owned by the early pioneers. Many of the neighborhoods and communities of the greater San Lorenzo area have been annexed by other cities throughout the years. Former properties of William Meek (the largest early San Lorenzo landowner), John and Eli Lewelling, Captain Roberts, Charles Stenzel, C. W. Hathaway, Otis Webb, and others are now located within city limits of San Leandro and Hayward or have become independent regions of unincorporated Eden Township in Alameda County.

There are many examples of these changes throughout the greater San Lorenzo area. Washington Manor homes, bordered by Washington Avenue, San Lorenzo Creek, and the bay, were annexed to San Leandro in May 1957. Residents of the Halcyon area, bordered by Washington Avenue and the Bayfair Mall property, voted for annexation in 1954. Also in the 1950s, the property bordered by Hesperian and Lewelling Boulevards and Washington Avenue was annexed to San Leandro. Even today, residents of these unincorporated areas that lie within San Leandro's postal area must pay a nonresidence fee for a library card.

William Meek's land holdings were subdivided into five sales sections named Meek Garden Tract, Colonial Acres, Meek Estate Orchards, Hayward Acres, and Meek Boulevard Tract. Only one of these subdivisions, Hayward Acres, remains today. The property surrounding Meekland Avenue to Mission Boulevard is called Cherryland and is currently an unincorporated area of Alameda County located within Hayward. Sections of the Ashland area, such as Fairmont Terrace above Foothill Boulevard, and Hillcrest Knolls, also above Foothill Boulevard by 150th Avenue, are in the unincorporated area of Eden Township in San Leandro.

Over the years, San Lorenzo has decreased in acreage due to annexation but increased in population. A freeway system by the Four Corners (once the town crossroads), a rapid-transit system, and many shopping centers have changed this prosperous rural farming community into a commuter town.

STREET SCENE, 1905. Poplar trees line East Fourteenth Street, which had many names in the past—de Anza, El Camino Real del Norte, County Road, and in Hayward, Castro Street. Now Hayward calls the street Mission Boulevard. By 1907, the original electric-car tracks running along the side were moved to the middle section of the street.

WEBB FARM AND FOUNTAIN. The road in front of the fountain looks down to East Fourteenth Street, where Otis Webb planted poplar trees. His house and 100-acre farmland stretched from 170th to 172nd Avenues, bordering the Lewelling family farm. His son Edward built a home on the William Meek property at Montgomery Street and Sunset Boulevard that is now privately owned.

EAST FOURTEENTH STREET, 1905. Bicyclists on double and single bicycles ride down the dirt street originally called de Anza Trail after Juan Baptista de Anza. He guided an expedition of more than 200 people and 1,000 head of cattle in 1775–1776 from Mexico to San Francisco. A small plaque is located in unincorporated Ashland on the west side of East Fourteenth Street by the de Anza Village Apartments.

ELECTRIC RAILWAY CAR. Construction of the Oakland, San Leandro and Hayward Electric Railway began in 1891. By 1892, 14.3 miles of track for the electric streetcar line between Oakland and Hayward had been laid along County Road, now East Fourteenth Street and Mission Boulevard. An electric railway car ran every half hour from 5:00 a.m. until midnight daily. In 1906, it became the Oakland Traction Company.

CAPTAIN OTIS WEBB.

Born in New Bedford, Massachusetts, in 1813, Otis Webb (left) went to sea at age 18 and later became a sea captain of his own whaling vessel. In 1849, he and his brother erected a trading store at what became Webb and Sacramento Streets in San Francisco. In 1871, retired Captain Webb bought 100 acres of farmland, which extended from what are now 170th to 172nd Avenues to the hills, cut by Foothill Boulevard. He planted fruit trees and grain. The Webb house (below) overlooked the orchard and poplar trees that lined East Fourteenth Street. Around 1933, the farm was subdivided into the El Portal tract. The youngest daughter, Harriet, married William Meek Jr. About 1925, Edward Otis Webb built a 16-room house, which is currently a senior rest home at Montgomery Street and Sunset Boulevard.

TOURNQUIST HOUSE, 1900S. Blanche Tournquist lived at this Lewelling Boulevard house off Washington Avenue. She settled in San Lorenzo in 1919 and taught first and second grades at the San Lorenzo Grammar School in the 1920s and Sunset Elementary School in the 1930s. Tournquist was born in 1885 in the Modoc County town of Lookout.

ASHLAND AREA MAP. The boundaries of the Ashland Fire Department formed this map in the 1970s and is used by the Ashland Community Association. The area has changed from farms and flower nurseries to housing tracts, apartments, townhouses, and various businesses. The freeways and Bay Area Rapid Transit (BART) aid in transportation for this populated community.

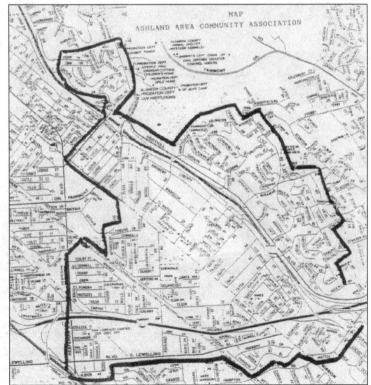

ASHLAND FIRE DEPARTMENT. Pictured are unidentified fireman with their "old red truck" and "new white trucks" in late 1940s. Prior to forming a department, volunteers would put out fires with buckets. With a community petition and the assistance of an Alameda County supervisor, a taxable district was formed in 1933. The first equipment was housed in a public garage until a station was built in 1938.

CHERRYLAND VOLUNTEER FIRE DEPARTMENT, 1945. Standing in front of Vic Hubbard's Garage on Meekland Avenue, the department began with, from left to right, Ed Foster, Jim Warjez, Caroll Johanson, Johnny Long, Frank Gomez, unidentified, Sal Strabroski, Tony Abreu, Orin Dennis, Ray LeBlanc, Frank Cordeira, Matt Silva, and Chief Vic Hubbard. The current fire department building at the corner of Grove Way and Meekland Avenue had a back entrance to Vic Hubbard's.

THE THOMFORD FAMILY. Standing in front of their car, from left to right, are Lucille, Andrew, Dorothy, and Muriel Thomford. They lived at 1010 Grove Way, between Western and Montgomery Avenues, across from the 1911 Burr house. Andrew was raised in Sunol and built the house (below) in 1924 on what used to be William Meek property. The lots were large, so they grew their own fruits and vegetables and raised poultry. Andrew's sister Doris married Jack Marlin of San Lorenzo. His grandfather, Henry Thomford, opened the Castro Valley Exchange in 1881, the first commercial business in Castro Valley. Dorothy lived in San Francisco until the 1906 earthquake and fire, which destroyed her family's house and forced them to move to Oakland. Lucille married Ray Lorge, whose family owned the California State Hatchery. She is Castro Valley's resident historian, coauthor of the Images of America book *Castro Valley*, and currently the McConaghy House manager.

ASHLAND AVENUE, 1920. Anna Francis and daughter Katherine stand at the front of the family home located southwest of the railroad tracks. Today BART trains travel high above the old tracks. Some of the neighbors in this area were the Furtado, Soto, Silva, Moura, Sequeira, and Frank Smith families.

FRANCIS PROPERTY, 1925. Alice Francis says good-bye to the family dog in her mother-in-law's backyard before leaving to visit relatives. The large yard with the shed and tank house in the background was Spotty's playground. Alice and her husband, Alfred, lived in a small house on Ashland Avenue next door to Anna Francis.

FRANCIS FAMILY INCREASES, 1928. Lorraine
Francis Repose holds baby niece Audrey
Marciel in the garden at Grandma Anna
Francis's house. The baby, daughter of Mamie
and Manuel Marciel, was born in the house on
Ashland Avenue. Today the property borders
Galway Drive, an entrance to the Hesperian
Gardens homes off Ashland Avenue.

OLD APRICOT ORCHARD. Maybelle Petersen leaves her parents' first house on the corner of
Montgomery Avenue and Grove Way during winter and walks west on Grove Way. The property
had been a part of William Meek's 2,000-acre estate, which was subdivided in 1911. Many
apricot trees, once part of Meek's orchards, remained on the land. The area was later annexed
to Hayward.

PETERSEN TEA PARTY. Two sisters, Alice and Maybelle (with ribbon in her hair), are having a tea party on the porch of their playhouse. Their father, Peter Petersen, built the playhouse before he constructed the large family house at 21492 Montgomery Avenue. The doll in the buggy was also invited to the tea party.

BUILDING THE SECOND HOUSE, 1926. Peter Petersen, a builder, replaced the first house, nickamed "a garage," on the corner of Montgomery Avenue and Grove Way. He was born in Newman, California, but his parents came from Als, Denmark, as did his wife, Helene. Chimneys, like the one already constructed on the front of the house, were important for heating houses during the 1920s.

PETERSEN FAMILY PHOTOGRAPH, 1928. Peter and Helene Petersen pose with their daughters, Doris, Maybelle, and Alice (from left to right), in front of their Montgomery Avenue house. The large double lot allowed for a cottage at the back of the property that borders Grove Street. Alice Petersen became a talented artist and lived in the house until her death in 2006. Sisters Maybelle Rasmussen and Doris Jones eventually sold the property.

SAN LORENZO FLOODING. Melvin Peters drives his General Motors pickup truck somewhere in the Washington Manor area. During heavy rains, the San Lorenzo Creek, lined with trees and plants, would overflow its dirt banks into the farmland west of Washington Avenue. The property owners sought assistance from the state and federal governments until a flood-control district was established.

HATHAWAY AVENUE HOUSE, 1945. Two-year-old Melvin Peters Jr. stands in front of his family's house that was recently moved from Grant Avenue to Hathaway Avenue in San Lorenzo. Many houses were demolished or moved when the David D. Bohannon Organization purchased the property to make the San Lorenzo Village. This house and barn are still located east of Blossom Way on Hathaway Avenue.

CHERRYLAND ORCHARD, 1911. Besse McCarty stands on the site of her future home on Blossom Way. Her husband, Edward, bought the one-acre parcel from Cherryland Inc., and Ethel Meek Montgomery signed the deed. This cherry orchard had been part of William Meek's property. Meek brought cherry trees from Oregon, raising 4,200 of them on his 260 acres of fruit trees. Known as Meekland, the area later became part of Cherryland.

McCarty Family Home. Donna Mae McCarty pedals beside the lush garden near the fishpond at her Cherryland home on Blossom Way. Many homes in the 1930s had fishponds. The vines of the grapes in the vineyard can be seen in the rear. With large lots, many families could raise their own fruits and vegetables.

An Unusual Winter, 1933. Donna Mae McCarty stands under icicles covering the arbor at the family's Blossom Way home in Cherryland. Tank houses were the only source of water for many families, and sometimes they overflowed. During this very cold winter, icicles were the result of one such overflow. Most gardens in the area lost much of their foliage due to the cold weather.

NINTH HOUSE IN CHERRYLAND, 1914. Edward E. McCarty and his brothers built this home on Blossom Way. Edward and wife, Besse, lived in the tank house while building their home. Typical of houses in the era, it sported a large front porch with elaborately designed pillars. Note the tall mailbox in front of the cherry tree.

ROBERT'S LANDING AREA, 1992. On a San Lorenzo history class field trip, the adult students walk from the Southern Pacific Tracks to the bay at the end of Lewelling Boulevard, formerly Robert's Landing Road. In 1906, 48 acres of Captain Roberts's estate was sold to the Trojan Power Company, which made explosives until 1963. In 1992, after many delays, the Heron Bay housing development was built in this area.

EDEN JAPANESE COMMUNITY CENTER. The original Ashland Gakuen Center, built in 1911 on land donated by Minoru Okada next to his nursery on Ashland Avenue in San Lorenzo, was condemned because two fires gutted the building. In 1962, the Japanese community built this community center on Elgin Street off Ashland Avenue. Like the previous Ashland Gakuen Center, the center preserves ethnic ties between Japan and the community.

FAIRMONT HOSPITAL OF ALAMEDA COUNTY. The first hospital began in 1864 and was moved to its present location on 124 acres fronting Foothill Boulevard in 1869. Later the acreage totaled 400 and was used for a dairy, poultry, and hog farm until 1955. Also located on the grounds was a cemetery. Other burials were in potter field areas at Mount. Calvary Cemetery in San Leandro and San Lorenzo Pioneer Cemetery.

LAST SAN LORENZO NURSERY. The Kawahara Nursery on Ashland Avenue, by St. John's Catholic Church, is the last of many area nurseries, including the Okada Brothers wholesale carnation nursery on Ashland Avenue. In 1950, Isami, or Sam, Kawahara bought three acres of land from the Moura family and built greenhouses to establish a bedding-plant nursery. Born in 1921 on his parents' strawberry farm at the corner of Hesperian Boulevard and Russell Road, now West Winton Avenue, Sam attended San Leandro High School. His sons, David and John, both graduates of San Lorenzo High School, own a 75-acre nursery in Morgan Hill, California, and ship some plants to the Ashland nursery. They also ship herbs, perennials, potted plants, and vegetables to northern California retailers.

PLANTING TOMATOES, 1933. Pictured above are two of the Vierra brothers' six horses, Chief and Prince, pulling the tomato planter. The brothers, George (driving) and Antone (planting), with Edna Stenzel observing, leased 250 acres where the Hayward Airport now stands from the Stenzel Estates Company, Inc. The Stenzel family also owned a large dairy and farm where Stenzel Park is located, fronting Wicks Boulevard. The image below shows the brothers and brother-in-law Leland Christensen (left) planting tomatoes. In the background is their Klyber truck. They grew corn, cucumbers for pickling, tomatoes, peas, rhubarb, hay, apricots, and pears from 1932 to 1939. George, his wife, Isabel, and their daughter Shirley lived in the house on the property.

PICKLE BARRELS, 1940s. These workers stand by barrels used to cure cucumbers. All are unidentified except for Viola Dutra Maciel and Helen Borba Mello (first and second in first row) and Bertha Smith Perry (far right, first row). In the 1920s, John Harr started a small pickle business at his grandfather's ranch on Hesperian Boulevard. Later he formed a company and built his Lady's Choice Pickling Plant on Winton Avenue in Hayward.

THE DUTRA FAMILY, 1911. Posing in front of their house on Ashland Avenue between Delano and East Fourteenth Street, from left to right, are (first row) Veronica, Manuel (holding dog), and Minnie; (second row) Viola, Tony with mother Francis, and Lena. On their two acres, they raised corn, apricots, and other fruit trees. In later years, the house burned while a roofing company occupied it.

SPEEDWAY, 1931, AND STADIUM, 1946. The Oakland Speedway was an oiled, one-mile dirt track built in 1931 on farmland leased from the Coelho family. Designed for automobile and motorcycle racing, with grandstands seating 25,000 people, it was located in what is now the Bayfair area of East Fourteenth Street and Hesperian Boulevard. The "Oakland" refers to the Oakland Speedway Association. The last race in 1941 was a 200-mile motorcycle competition. Later that year, the grandstands burned. In 1942, the federal government banned all forms of auto racing under wartime restrictions. After the war, a new Oakland Stadium was built with a five-eighths track and a quarter-mile track on the same site. The first races were held on June 30, 1946. The stadium hosted roadsters, hardtops, sprint, midget, and stock cars for nine years until closing in 1955 for the construction of Bayfair Shopping Center.

ASHLAND HOLY GHOST ASSOCIATION HALL. The Holy Ghost Association of Ashland and San Lorenzo was incorporated on March 26, 1897. The purpose was to continue the traditions of the Portuguese and the dedication and devotion to the Holy Spirit. Many Portuguese from the Azores and Maderia Islands settled in the Ashland area of San Lorenzo. They continued the tradition of the Holy Ghost Celebration by holding a parade, mass, and a feast of sopas (above). It is held yearly in June at the hall located on Kent Avenue (below). The IDES, Irnandade do Divino Espirito Santo, a Portuguese fraternal society, also has meetings in the hall.

Four

SAN LORENZO SCHOOLS

The San Lorenzo Unified School District is one of the oldest continuously operating school systems in the state of California. From a humble beginning in 1850 with only six students in a tiny, portable building shared with Hayward, the district reached its peak in 1970 with 18,000 students enrolled in 28 schools.

On November 8, 1859, San Lorenzo Elementary School District, with one school, was established. With increased enrollment in 1902, a larger two-story wooden building replaced the school. Unfortunately, in 1928, an arsonist destroyed the building. In 1929, the community quickly built a two-story brick school, also housing the district office, that fronted Usher Street. During this time, Ashland (1923) and Sunset (1926) were built, creating three schools until 1945. The first school board, organized in 1864, was made up of members William Meek, John Lewelling, and Albert E. Crane.

With an increased population in the 1940s, the school building boom began with Village School (1945), David E. Martin (1947), and then Fairmont (1948). All five schools were elementary level. Beginning in 1949, grades seven and eight began attending junior highs such as David D. Bohannon (1949), Edendale (1950), Washington Manor (1952), and then Barrett (1958).

The first school-site building, San Lorenzo, was declared unsafe for students in 1952, so they attended the new Hesperian School. San Lorenzo Elementary School District offices remained until 1972, when the building was replaced.

In 1952, more elementary schools were needed, so Halcyon, Lewelling, Grant, Colonial Acres, Corvallis, Dayton, Del Rey, El Portal, Fairmont Terrace, Linda Vista, Bay, Hillside, and Argonne were built. Russell School joined the district in 1957 and Halcyon was annexed to San Leandro in 1954.

All high-school students attended Hayward Union High School until San Lorenzo and Arroyo High were built. In 1963, the school-district residents voted to annex them into the district, creating the San Lorenzo Unified School District. Many changes have occurred since, as schools were sold or leased, Marina High was built, and grade levels were rearranged. Currently there are nine elementary schools (kindergarten through fifth), three middle schools (sixth through eighth), three high schools (with a district enrollment of 12,000), and one adult school.

SAN LORENZO PUBLIC SCHOOL, 1800S. After sharing a portable schoolhouse with Hayward for six to eight students, San Lorenzo settlers built this permanent school (above) in 1850 on the site behind the present-day Usher Street San Lorenzo Unified School District offices. The students traveled to school on dirt roads that were muddy and full of chuckholes in winter and dusty in summer if the water wagon was elsewhere. The 1877 school census listed 201 children between 5 and 17 years of age attending San Lorenzo Public School and 62 of the same age not attending during the school year. The 46 children in this 1890 school photograph (below) are unidentified except for the author's grandfather (fifth from the left, top row).

SAN LORENZO PUBLIC SCHOOL. This two-story wooden structure (above) replaced the small school in 1902. Unfortunately, in 1928, it burned to the ground due to an arsonist. In 1911, there were 265 students and seven teachers. Young Dorothy Gansberger of San Lorenzo wrote a prize-winning essay stating, "The town is lighted with electricity and has an up-to-date telephone system." She became the principal of Village School in 1948. The class of 1922 (below) rode the streetcar on a Saturday to Oakland to take this photograph. Principal Clyde Lawson is seated in the center of the first row. The fifth student from the left in the first row is Pauline Joseph, the author's mother. Irma Quigley, the sixth student from the left in the second row, was hired later by Clyde Lawson to teach at Ashland School.

SCHOOL AND ADMINISTRATIVE OFFICES. This brick building above replaced the wooden school that burned in 1928 on the same site as the present-day Usher Street San Lorenzo Unified School District offices. The school contained kindergarten through the eighth grade and the administrative offices from 1929 to 1952, before it was declared unsafe for students because of not being earthquake proof and having no second-floor fire escape. The San Lorenzo School District offices occupied the structure until 1972, when the current fort-style building replaced it. "Unified" was added to the name in 1963 after the Hayward Union High School District discontinued. San Lorenzo and Arroyo High Schools became part of the elementary district. The first school board of trustees in 1859 had three members. From 1941 to 1948, J. P. Joseph Jr. (below) was one of the three school trustees. In 1955, it changed to five elected members.

Re-Elect...

J. P. Joseph, Jr.

School Trustee

San Lorenzo School District
Incumbent

VOTE FOR HIM MAY 15, 1942

SAN LORENZO SCHOOL. The last eighth-grade class to graduate from this school building (above) sits in front of the 1929 brick structure. Seated in the front row, far left is the author, and principal True Tourtillot and teacher Doris Kalik are seventh and eighth from the left in the front row. The school became the district office until it was demolished in 1972 for a new administration building. Hesperian School, on Drew Street off of Hesperian Boulevard, became the new school for kindergarten through sixth-grade students. The seventh- and eighth-grade students attended Edendale Junior High on Ashland Avenue. Below, in 1938, class photographs were taken with the school building above the photograph. These fourth-, fifth-, and sixth-grade classes are seated in front of a large tree planted by superintendent Clyde Lawson.

SAN LORENZO CLASSES, 1800s. The 32 students of the receiving class of 1898 (above) are attending their first year of school at the small San Lorenzo Public School located by the entrance to the now maintenance yards of San Lorenzo District offices. These names are not according to placement but convey the pioneer families of this time: Annie Rippe, Mary Rodgers, Alice Hill, Maud Marlin, Neely Roto, Lallie Soito, Mary George, Peter Jorgensen, Hattie Joseph, Maud Wells, Hazel King, Hazel Burke, Nick Jorgesen, Edith Shellmadine, Rita Ferry, Nellie Forth, Ernest Stalden, Oscar Soito, Nora Sole, Helga Jacobson, Mary Cardoza, Sophie Perry, Elsie Perry, Lydia Lovera, Manuel Terry, Fred Rippe, Ruphene Tavario, Charles Rota, Annie Nominee, Dora Rippe, Maggie Dutra, and Maggie Silva. This 1897 photograph (below) is at the same school. Note the unexpressive faces of the students and the footwear.

RUSSELL PUBLIC SCHOOL. The first school in the Danish farm community of Russell City (above) was built in 1895 and named after Joel Russell, an Englishman from Maine. Located on Russell Road, now West Winton Avenue, it was a one-school district. In 1940, it was demolished and a new school (below) was constructed by the Works Project Administration. On November 27, 1957, by a vote of four to one, the voters of the Russell School District voted to liquidate the district and become part of the San Lorenzo School District. The annexation occurred in July 1957. As the 22nd school in the San Lorenzo system, with 350 students, 10 teachers, and 6 classified employees, it continued as an elementary school. In the late 1970s, it became Russell High School until it was sold in 1980 for the Hayward Business Park.

SAN LORENZO GRAMMAR SCHOOL, 1927. Some students in this third-grade photograph are Al Nicolotti, John Ogeles, Stanley Silva, Frank Azevado, John Pinetta, Laura Moura, Lora Tamask, and Helen Ogeles. When Max Baer, a San Lorenzo School graduate, became boxing's heavyweight champion of the world, he visited principal Clyde Lawson and this class. The school burned in the summer of 1928, so portable buildings were used for one year.

SUNSET ELEMENTARY SCHOOL. The third school of the San Lorenzo Elementary School District was built in 1926 and located by the corner of Royal and Sunset Avenues in the Hayward Acres area off Hesperian Boulevard. In 1955, nine classrooms, the multipurpose room, and the administrative unit were replaced, and the physically handicapped unit was integrated into the school in 1956. Today it is the Royal Sunset High School.

ASHLAND SCHOOL. The second school in San Lorenzo, built in 1923 facing East Fourteenth Street (above), was named for the Ashland area, an unincorporated section between the cities of Hayward and San Leandro. Ashland itself was named for the Oregon ash trees growing there. Superintendent Clyde Lawson, principal at San Lorenzo School since 1914, now had a two-school district. High-school students attended Hayward Union High School. In 1954, the State Division of Architecture declared the original building structurally inadequate. New classrooms, a multipurpose room, and an administrative unit replaced it in 1979. The students moved to Edendale Junior High School due to a reconfiguration of the grades, as middle schools were eliminated. The school was demolished for apartments. An aerial view (below) shows East Fourteenth Street in the foreground, Kent Avenue at the top, and Henry's Market at the far right.

SAN LORENZO ADMINISTRATION BUILDING, 1950S. From 1929 to 1952, this brick building housed students from kindergarten through the eighth grade and the San Lorenzo Elementary School District office. From 1952 to 1972, it was only the district office. The Quonset hut warehouse is in the maintenance yard. At left is the San Lorenzo Cemetery and College Street. In the upper left corner, the houses are on the former San Lorenzo Grove property.

SAN LORENZO SUPERINTENDENTS. In this original compilation photograph (clockwise, from top left) are William Dolph, Clyde Lawson, Dr. Alan Badal, and Paul Ehret. Clyde Lawson was teacher, principal, and superintendent from 1914 until 1948. Paul Ehret led a district of six schools in 1948 to 28 schools in 1975. William Dolph (1975–1978) and Alden Badal (1978–1992) made the difficult decisions to close schools and reorganize grade levels.

DAVID E. MARTIN SCHOOL.
Named for the Alameda
County superintendent of
schools in 1947, this became
the sixth school in the district.
Known simply as Martin
School, it is located at the end
of Paseo Grande and formerly
contained the Wes Gordon
Science Museum. Additions
were added in 1958 as the
population increased. Closed in
1982, the facility is now leased
to a private school.

FAIRMONT ELEMENTARY SCHOOL. The fifth elementary school in the San Lorenzo School District was built in 1948, when district enrollment was 2,732 students. This aerial view shows 150th Avenue at the bottom and the area for the 580 Freeway at right. In 1979, the school was demolished for the exit to 150th Avenue.

THIS AWARD

IS MADE TO THE MEMBERS OF

San Lorenzo Elementary School
San Lorenzo, California

OVER 90% OF WHOM

ARE BUYING U. S. WAR BONDS THROUGH

A SYSTEMATIC PURCHASE PLAN

Henry Morgenthau Jr.
SECRETARY OF THE TREASURY

STATE CHAIRMAN

STATE ADMINISTRATOR

UNITED STATES WAR BONDS. In 1942, an award was given to the San Lorenzo Elementary School by the California secretary of the treasury, Henry Morgenthan Jr., for participating in the war-bond program. During World War II, 93 former graduates of San Lorenzo Elementary School were in the service. Their names are on the San Lorenzo All Wars Memorial by Village Realtors, fronting Grant Avenue.

GRANT SCHOOL, 1952. Built on the Terkelsen farm after the last crops were harvested, Grant was one of five new elementary schools built at this time in the San Lorenzo School District, which totaled 16 schools with an enrollment of 8,392 students. Katherine Zachariades became the first principal. It closed in the fall of 1977 due to declining enrollment and was leased until reopening in the 1990s for elementary students.

VILLAGE SCHOOL, 1945. When David D. Bohannon built the first village houses, he left space for churches, a shopping plaza, and schools (above). In 1945, with 1,329 homes and three schools (San Lorenzo, Ashland, and Sunset) already in the San Lorenzo Village, the Village School (below) was built facing Hesperian Boulevard by the shopping plaza. Dorothy Gansberger, the first principal, began her teaching career in 1921 at San Lorenzo School where she had been a student. By 1924, she was teaching in Oakland, but she returned to San Lorenzo in 1944. Dorothy wrote and spoke about San Lorenzo history, and "The Story of San Lorenzo" is Elizabeth Brook's adaptation of Dorothy's presentation to students. Dorothy's family lived where Faria's Hardware store was located on Manor Boulevard, formerly Gansberger Road. Village School became the Eden Area Regional Occupational Center in 1973 and was later sold for businesses and townhouses.

DAVID D. BOHANNON SCHOOL, 1949. At the dedication of the junior high school named in his honor is David D. Bohannon (left), a significant figure in the Bay Area and well known among his peers on a national scale for the San Lorenzo Village development. In his lifetime he built a total of 26,000 homes, 136 subdivisions, and 360 acres of commercial property. The Sea Scouts (below) formed a color guard, as the Village Scouts raised the flag over the school facing Bockman Road. In the 1980s, Bohannon Junior High changed to Bohannon High School and housed three museums: Wes Gordon Science, San Lorenzo Schools, and the Native American. The junior-high students attended either a high school or elementary school. Since 1998, it has been the Bohannon Middle School, with sixth- through eighth-grade students attending.

SAN LORENZO HIGH SCHOOL.
Groundbreaking ceremonies occurred
on January 24, 1950 (right). Standing
in front of the sign, from left to right,
are Bob Coat; Lloyd Blair, assistant
superintendent of San Lorenzo
Elementary School District; contractor
Mr. Burrows; W. Bonetti; and architect
G. Simonds. All students attended
Hayward Union High School before San
Lorenzo opened in 1950 with freshman
and sophomores. Built on a former
apricot orchard and fruit dryer owned
by Jack Smith on Lewelling Boulevard,
it became a full four-year high school in
1952. The faculty from Hayward High
School autographed an image of the
school below. Among the signatures
are those of principal Carl Ekoos, vice
principal Nels Nelson, Martha Watson,
Marcella Clancy, Vincent Lamb,
Josephine Williams, Alden Cook, Arta
Williams, Clementina Vaz, Lorraine
Bollinger, Lawrence Anderson, James
Frank, Tony Winn, and Paul Smith.

121

MARINA HIGH SCHOOL, 1964. This high school, fronting Wicks Boulevard in Washington Manor area, was built by the San Lorenzo Unified School District in 1964 and sold in 1982. All buildings were demolished except the multiuse room, now the Marina Recreation Center. The area was annexed to San Leandro in the 1950s, but the following schools remained in the San Lorenzo District: Corvallis, Dayton, Washington Manor, and Lewelling.

SAN LORENZO SCHOOLS INSTITUTE, 1967. Pictured here, from left to right, are speaker Dan Moore, school-board member Corinne Aitken, school-board member Georgia Henderson, and Larry Reineike. Certificated staff attended the institute. Corinne Aitken, the first woman elected to the San Lorenzo School Board in 1954, was a former teacher and was reelected for many terms. Her husband, Kenneth Aitken, served on the Hayward Area Recreation and Park District board.

REBELS FOOTBALL BILLBOARD. Advertising San Lorenzo High School football on this billboard on Lewelling Boulevard was one way to publicize. Recently a sports Hall of Fame was established at the high school to honor championship teams, coaches, and outstanding sports players. Honored were the 1955 and 1977 football squads (three coaches and 18 athletes) for winning Athletic League championships. Some inductees became college and professional football players.

BOXER, MAX BAER. Boxing's heavyweight champion of the world in 1934 and 1935 (left) graduated from San Lorenzo Elementary School in the 1920s. The Jacob Baer family lived in many places, including San Lorenzo, and the Baers often visited their good friends, the Holdeners, in Russell City. When Max, the champion, came home to his Hesperian Boulevard house, he visited his friends in Russell City, driving his bright yellow convertible Cadillac.

SAN LORENZO DISTRICT CONFERENCE ROOM. The 1984 board of education, from left to right, are (first row) superintendent Dr. Alden Badal and Pat Griffin; (second row) Betty Moose, Harry Gin, Loren Simpson, and Dorothy Partridge. The clay mural on the wall was made by Evelyn Jones's Bohannon Junior High School class for the bicentennial and depicts United States historical events on various-sized clay tablets.

SAN LORENZO CEMETERY, 1992. Teubert Smith (left) and Steven MacDonald carry a small gravestone found outside the gate on a history class field trip to the San Lorenzo Pioneer Cemetery. By using the *San Lorenzo Cemetery Booklet*, which contains a map and listing of the burials, the class was able to place the gravestone on the proper grave site.

SAN LORENZO SCHOOLS MUSEUM. In 1984, along with the late Shirley Johanson, Marcene Willard and Barbara Kuhns (seated) organized the San Lorenzo Schools Museum, which was housed at Bohannon High School until 1992. The project was the joint effort of the San Lorenzo Unified School District and the San Lorenzo Council of the Parent Teacher Association. A San Lorenzo history class, taught by the author, was held in the museum.

SAN LORENZO SCHOOLS MUSEUM, 1986. Two San Lorenzo natives, Elvira Terkelsen Woodward and William Teubert Smith, discuss the old days at the San Lorenzo history class held in the museum. Elvira's family owned the property where Grant School is now located on Grant Avenue. Teubert's father owned and operated the last blacksmith shop on Albion Avenue. They both graduated from the San Lorenzo Elementary School and Hayward High School.

SCHOOLS MUSEUM SIGN. In 1986, Ray Anderson made this sign in the Adult School (formerly Linda Vista School) woodworking class for the San Lorenzo Schools Museum, located at Bohannon High School next door. The museum contained images and artifacts from all the schools, including ones that had been demolished or closed. It also contained a raised platform made by Marina High's woodworking class on which to place old school desks.

SAN LORENZO HISTORY CLASS. Pictured here, from left to right, are teacher Charlotte Davis (standing), an unidentified teacher, teacher Rebecca Calderwood, teacher Roz Weiss, and San Lorenzo Village Homes Association administrator Nancy Van Huffel. The San Lorenzo School's third- and fourth-grade teachers attended the author's history classes where guests, movies, images, and a bus field trip conveyed the history of San Lorenzo.

BIBLIOGRAPHY

Baker, Joseph E., ed. *History of Alameda County California, Volume II: Biographical.* Chicago: The S. J. Clarke Publishing Company, 1928.

Eden Writers. *Hayward . . . The First 100 Years.* Hayward, CA: Hayward Centennials Committee, 1975.

Hall, Harwood. *Eden Township: Its Agriculture.* Hayward, CA: Hayward Area Historical Society and Lois Over, 1997.

Hayward Area Historical, and Hayward Area Genealogical Societies. *San Lorenzo Cemetery Booklet.* Hayward, CA: Hayward Area Historical Society, 1988.

Marciel, Doris. *San Lorenzo A to Z.* Hayward, CA: Hayward Area Historical Society, 2004.

Motter, Tom. *A History of the Oakland Speedway 1931–1941, Volume I: Tracks of the West.* Rancho Cordova, CA: Vintage Images, 2002.

———. *A History of the Oakland Stadium 1946–1955, Volume II: Tracks of the West.* Rancho Cordova, CA: Vintage Images, 2001.

New Historical Atlas of Alameda County, California. Oakland, CA: Thompson and West, 1878; reprint, Fresno, CA: Valley Publishers, 1976.

Sandoval, John. *The Rancho of Don Guillermo Volume I, The Early Years: 1843–1890.* Hayward, CA: Mount Eden Historical Publishers, 1991.

Social Studies Classes at Sunset High School, McDow, Mildred, ed. *A History of Hayward.* Hayward, CA: Mildred McDow, 1970.

Thoman, Ivy Rose. *A History of St Johns Catholic Church (1897–1972).* San Lorenzo, CA: Ivy Rose Thoman.

Wilkinson, Chet and Nola Coding. *A History of San Lorenzo Community Church (1874–1982).* San Lorenzo, CA: San Lorenzo Community Church.

Visit us at
arcadiapublishing.com